1000 LIVING DETAILS

1000 LIVING DETAILS

Cristina Paredes Benítez

LOFT

1000 Living Details

Loft Publications, S.L.
Via Laietana 32, 4°, of. 92
08003 Barcelona, España
Tel.: +34 93 268 80 88
Fax: +34 93 268 70 73
loft@loftpublications.com
www.loftpublications.com

Editorial coordinator:
Simone K. Schleifer

Assistant to editorial coordination:
Aitana Lleonart Triquell

Editor and text:
Cristina Paredes Benítez

Translation:
Cillero & de Motta

Art director:
Mireia Casanovas Soley

Design and layout coordination:
Claudia Martínez Alonso

Cover layout:
María Eugenia Castell Carballo

Layout:
Cristina Simó Perales

© 2011 Loft Publications

ISBN: 978-84-9936-857-3

Printed in Spain

INTRODUCTION

This is not just another book on interior decorating. The chapters in this book do not discuss styles or trends. Neither are they intended to be merely a list of products. The aim of this work is to present 1000 ideas for organizing and planning your home, for feeling comfortable in it and for satisfying the needs of everyday life. The topics presented here concern the organization of space and access, showing the differences between natural and artificial lighting, along with the real and current options available regarding sustainability and environmental issues. Whether you want to start from scratch or just carry out a few alterations to your present home, this book is intended to help you make your property more functional. So that our home adapts to our needs and not the other way around.

These 1000 details are presented in various different ways: as tips on what type of paving to lay in each place and why, or examples of how the lighting has been designed for a particular house. There are also brief explanations or clarifications of concepts that may be helpful to readers, such as explaining what a hydroponic green roof is, or what to take into account when planning an electrical installation.

The chapter on organizing spaces, for instance, is intended to act as a guide for the reader to help them discover which architectural features are most suited to their home and lifestyle. Unique spaces, mezzanine floors or separations between day and night areas are some of the topics illustrated here. The book also looks at those areas in the house that connect up the various rooms and define the movements carried out in the home, unveiling the personality of its occupants: stairways, hallways leading outdoors, corridors, etc.

The furniture, which is an essential feature of the home, defines each room, throwing light on the personality of the owners, and is one of the most useful ways of making the most of the space, which at times can be quite limited. This part provides an overview of the subject with illustrated examples of built-in shelving, made-to-measure modular furniture or storage applications.

An attempt has also been made to devote part of the book to floors, walls, ceilings and roofs, which are often passed over in books on interior decorating. The differences in materials and applications are clarified, showing the various options that are available so that the most appropriate can be chosen in each case. This is important for defining the appearance and use of a room. Real examples are shown for different surfaces and finishes in various rooms to help the reader decide. Doors and windows are given a separate chapter, with some useful tips and visual ideas.

Aware that outdoor living areas are just as important as those inside, the opportunity was seized on to analyze the strategies that might help people to enjoy life outdoors even more. From the use of a porch to the paths that can be created in a garden, this chapter offers solutions for making the most of patios, landscaping terraces or improving privacy on apartment balconies.

Color and lighting are key elements that can be resolved cheaply with very little effort. Changing the lights in a room or the color of a wall is not expensive and can give a whole new take on the place. In these sections there are some interesting examples and ideas of how to choose the most appropriate lighting, what drapes or blinds best suit our needs or how to transform the look of a place with the application of color.

Renovating a home, whether just carrying out slight alterations to the layout of an apartment or completely refurbishing a historic building, are a world apart in architectural terms. Functionality and aesthetics need to come together to generate living spaces that are practical and attractive at the same time. The chapter devoted to this subject offers examples of all cases, including both the simplest solutions and advice on how to maintain the original character of older properties.

The section on saving natural resources (one of the most extensive) looks at the issues involved in making a home more sustainable and what tools are available to homeowners to make it more efficient. Active systems, involving the installation of solar panels, wind turbines, heaters, etc. are treated separately from passive systems. The latter attempt to enhance the air-conditioning and lighting systems by combining the sun and breeze with good orientation, insulation and cross ventilation systems. This chapter is complemented by another on eco-materials with information to help the reader make the right choice, by illustrating the differences between natural, recycled and recyclable materials.

Apart from the information on the use of water in the chapter on saving natural resources, the book has a section specifically devoted to swimming pools, fountains and all those elements, albeit decorative or functional, where water is the main focus. Here you will find details that will help you decide where and how to install your pool, along with examples of ponds or fountains installed both in and outside the house. There are also illustrations of domestic spas and ideas for fittings and plumbing installations.

Finally, the last chapter touches on a trend that has now become a reality: new technologies in the home. Domotics or technologies associated with entertainment and leisure are briefly presented with examples of motorized elements and rooms reserved for watching movies or playing on the console.

In short, the book offers 1000 details, 1000 snippets of information, thus becoming a tool that invites reflection and is essential for being able to make informed choices.

0001 Prefabricated spaces are an ecological and economical option. In this prototype, a single room has been designed where the bathroom and kitchen share part of the space and where the bedroom has privacy.

0002 To avoid separating elements, one solution is to combine different functions, such as cooking and eating, in the same space. Take advantage of every corner in the home to distribute the different uses so that each one has a defined area in a corner of the house.

0003 This small space has been converted into an apartment with one area. In these homes, it is important to leave a clear central area to multiply the uses of the small surface area.

0004 This single, long space was transformed into a loft with two different ambiences: work/exhibition space and private area. This division was achieved by concentrating the different uses at both ends and using the kitchen as a link.

0005 A good idea to save space in studio environments is to unify the style with simple furnishings and integrate it into the decoration of the house.

0006 When designing a home as a studio space, why not have some lightweight partitions, such as panels or sliding doors, if necessary, to maintain the privacy of the occupants in the bedroom or bathroom.

0007 Prefabricated buildings create more flexible spaces; they are designed to provide all rooms with minimal resources. In this case, for example, the different floor covering materials separate the rooms.

0008 Studio spaces and their lack of unnecessary divisions, especially when it comes to partitions or high walls, promote greater mobility and visibility. Small homes and loft apartments are the main beneficiaries of this solution.

0001

0002

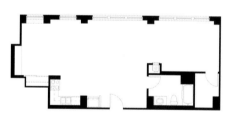
Floor plan

0003

0004

Floor plan

0005

3D Representation

Floor plan

0006

Floor plan

0007

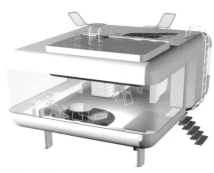

3D Representation

0008

0009 The natural distribution of spaces, contemporary furnishings and a trowelled concrete floor are the elements that have been used to achieve an interior with high spatial coherence in this small apartment in Miami.

0010 One of the advantages of the studio homes is the flexibility. Except for bathrooms and kitchens that need water and drainage facilities, the remaining spaces can be organized in many ways and changed at the owner's discretion.

0011 The bathroom and kitchen of this apartment are hidden behind a wall lined with fabric. The result is a studio space in which some logs and a bathtub are prominent decorative features and are integrated into the room.

0012 This apartment combines different solutions: a mezzanine and steps to differentiate levels and to achieve a unique modern and dynamic appearance.

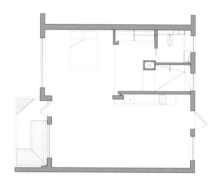

Floor plan

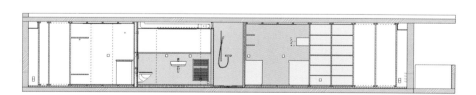

Section

0013

Floor plan

0014

0015

0016

0013 Adding a piece of furniture or decorative and functional accessory as the centerpiece of the home is a solution to manage the distribution of the spaces, especially in one-room apartments.

0014 The pinpoint distribution of the spaces is the best choice for small studio environments such as this one measuring 31.5 m² (339 ft²), where every corner is a closet and the furniture is multi-functional.

0015 To increase the feeling of spaciousness in a studio space, install low cabinets and equip the interior in an austere way as possible. In this way the spaces do not seem cluttered and you achieve the impression of a large and bright interior.

0016 Small homes can be designed in the format of a studio. In this way they gain in size and comfort for day to day activity. A small home is the most suitable option for single people or couples, as they do not require as much space or privacy.

0017 In this light and spacious environment, the original pillars intuitively define the different areas (kitchen, living room and bedroom).

0018 Joining several areas of a house in a single space is an ideal solution for the living area. This home is a perfect example: kitchen, dining room and library are on the same floor. The family can spend time together throughout the day.

0019 One of the most common options to improve communication in a home is to unite the public space in one area. Typically this area combines the dining room, kitchen and living room, so that all people who do not require privacy may come together in this space.

0020 Lighting, preferably natural, creates a greater feeling of spaciousness. The glass wall in this annex that is used as a separate home serves this purpose.

0021 The most obvious advantages in an open space distribution are that it promotes communication between the different areas, activities are multiplied and actions that are normally assigned to each room are mixed.

Floor plan

0019

Floor plan

0020

0021

0022 The almost full opening of the glass walls that limit the living room fuses the boundaries between the interior and exterior, which is only differentiated by the change of materials in the floor covering and the textile panels surrounding the residence.

0023 A half wall separates the living room from the kitchen. This partition hides part of the kitchen and keeps the cooking appliances and other kitchen equipment out of sight. This option unifies spaces without breaking the homogeneity of the decorative style.

0024 To make the space of this apartment in New York more flexible, most of the walls were torn down. The result is single, open and bright room; sliding panels were installed allowing you to change the distribution.

Floor plan

0025

Floor plan

0026

0027

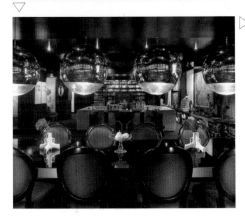

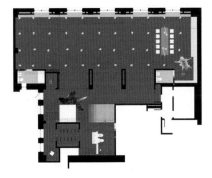

Floor plan

0025 By converting the bathroom into the only en-closed space in the studio, a centerpiece has been cre-ated around it which organizes the other uses without structural constraints.

0026 A good way to open the spaces in a home is to install movable walls. In this house by Barton Myers Associates, an original steel and glass wall has been built that slides with a mechanism similar to garage doors so that they space can open up with the exte-rior patio.

0027 The library, living room and dining area share the central area of the apartment. The black color of the walls unifies this single room which has different uses.

0030

0031

0032

Floor plan

0028 This impressive high-rise space is transformed into a boundless room through the use of hangar doors. These movable walls are the best option to improve the interior and exterior connection.

0029 This space containing the kitchen, dining room and living room, has been enlarged through the use of mirror on one of the walls of the apartment. This solution is used to gain light and not to saturate an area that that has three different uses.

0030 To maximize the space in this small apartment, the kitchen has been combined with the dining and living room without erecting walls that reduce the size of the rooms. A closet that also serves as a wall completes the organization of this open space.

0031 Furniture can organize the location of the rooms. A long wooden bench and colorful floor lamp are used to separate one of the bedrooms, which has a minimalist-Nordic style, and a small retro-style living room.

0032 In the refurbishment of this apartment the partition walls have been torn down to open up the space. With this change and the continuity of the wooden floor, the kitchen and living room are connected. The fireplace, open on both sides, is the heart of the new space.

0033 If the house has an interior courtyard position the living areas next to it to gain natural light and ventilation, as has been done in this house, where the kitchen, living room and bedroom are situated around a sunny patio.

0034 The layout of the rooms can be carried out with a specific distribution of furniture. In this case, the dining table is the element that separates the kitchen area and living room. The result is an interior which facilitates communication and serves for both activities.

0035 In this home, a small pool has been installed on the balcony, next to the living area. This solution allows the family to gather in the same space even if they are all carrying out different activities.

0036 In this case, an undulating design is the best solution to separate private rooms from common rooms, as shown in the plan. Furthermore, the bedrooms can be situated at both ends, which increases privacy.

0037 The distribution of this loft provides great flexibility and fluidity of movement between each of the rooms. The dining area and living room, besides sharing the same space, are unified through bespoke furniture.

0038 The study in this home is located on the lower level of the house, which is a quieter space. Despite this, it accesses the exterior through the garden and access to ground floor via stairs.

Floor plan

Floor plans

0036

Site plan

0037

0038

0039 This unusual home proposes an alternative in the organization of spaces and breaks monotony with unusual items, along with the original bedroom a pink meditation room has been installed.

0040 When designing where the different rooms should be located, the architects chose a more private space for the outdoor dining area and a stylish garden.

0041 If a home has a library or study, take into account the location in relation to other potentially noisy or busier rooms. A good option is to place it next to the bedrooms or in a wing away from the living area.

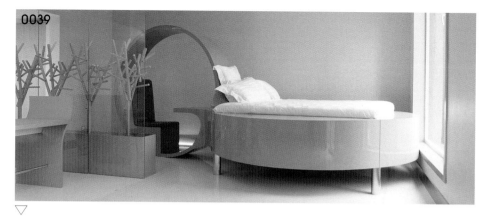

0042

0043

Floor plan

0044

0042 The home stands out for its unique location on the site affecting the design and layout of the rooms. In these cases the lighting solutions and openings are not normally conventional.

0043 The space requirements of a family can vary. To achieve a flexible layout and optimize the space, have a hub where the bathroom and kitchen are located, and leave a free surrounding space to distribute the other rooms.

0044 One of the most important decisions regarding the layout of rooms is the views. The owners can choose which spaces will enjoy the best views in terms of their preferences: living room, bedroom, study...

0045 Whenever possible, rooms should be grouped together according to their use in living and sleeping areas. For example, the living room can be located next to the dining room and the kitchen and bedrooms can be moved to another location. In this case, the entrance and reception room separate these two areas.

0046 Color can be used to define the layout of spaces. Green has been used in a volume located between the kitchen and reception area and defines the border between the different spaces without partitions.

0047 So as not to occupy space required for other rooms various functions can be distributed in the same room. Here, for example, the study area is positioned above the headboard.

0048 Color can be a determining factor in the layout of spaces. A central block of black in this Parisian apartment serves to divide the main living area from the private areas.

0045

Floor plan

0046

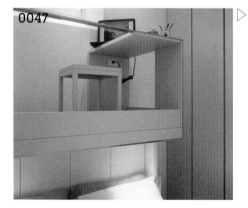

0047

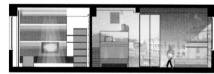

Section

0048

Floor plan and section

0049

0050

0051

0049 This prototype shows how through the good layout of spaces in this house of 19 m² (204 ft²) can contain four basic rooms; the solution is to distribute the rooms at various levels and multiply their uses.

0050 The organization of the spaces depends on the slope of the lots or the location of a house. In this houseboat, the living area is on the top floor, which is accessed by a bridge, which has views of the landscape.

0051 The various functions of the house, such as kitchen, bedrooms or bathroom, have been distributed in satellite modules around the main volume, where the living room is located. This network distribution saves space in prefab houses.

0052

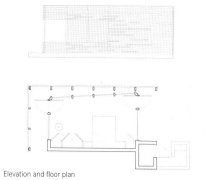

Elevation and floor plan

0053

0054

Floor plan

0055

Floor plans

0056

0057

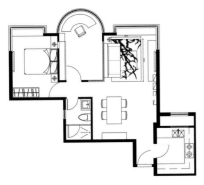

Floor plan

0052 In the annexes or cabins located in natural areas the layout options are extremely clear: the main space, whether it is the living room or bedroom, should be clearly facing the landscape and natural environment.

0053 The location of the bathroom and Jacuzzi on the first floor and along with the glass façade reflects the desire of owners to be able to enjoy a bath and the relaxing views of the Pacific Ocean at the same time.

0054 In this summerhouse the rooms have been distributed according to the priorities of owners, the bedrooms are smaller to give more space to the common area, which is used more.

0055 This home has been distributed according to a regular modular division of space. Depending on the needs of each room more or less modules are used, the same surface area is not required for a living room than for a bathroom or bedroom.

0056 To position the kitchen in the desired location and achieve an open distribution the facilities have been left in full view, which achieves an industrial aesthetic.

0057 By tearing down a wall in the apartment and replacing it with a fixed glass expanse two improvements are made: increased natural lighting in the living room and the study is visually unified with the rest of the house.

0058 Screens or fabrics are an effective and practical solution to separate rooms in a home, especially if one space has multiple uses. It is also an easily reversible solution, as virtually no installation is required.

0059 Panels that resemble the Japanese *shoji* are the solution used in this apartment to separate the bedroom area from the living room. As they are mobile, they can be opened and the two spaces can become one.

0060 Movable panels define the layout of the openings available in this home. By moving these elements you can completely transform the appearance of the house and its spaces are not only related to the interior but they are also connected with the garden.

0061 Elegant glass expanses that slide on rails in the floor mark a subtle separation between the different rooms in the home on the Australian coast.

0062 To separate rooms or uses within a modern loft without losing its originality, the best option is to install light and movable partitions, such as these white curtains. In this way, the interiors are kept in order without visually cluttering the space.

0063 A simple succession of glazed windows forms a separation between the hallway and bedrooms and the bathroom. This option breaks the monotony of the interior, clad almost entirely in wood.

0058

0059

0060

0061

0062

0063

0064 Partitions can be walls, soffits, sliding doors and even furniture, as in this Dutch home. The closet, in addition to containing the fire and a bookcase, serves as a screen that separates the room from the staircase.

0065 Glass partitions have many advantages: easy to install and allows light to pass. In this apartment by Filippo Bombace, a colored glass partition has been used to separate the reception area from the rest of the house.

0066 Mobile divisions are perfect to have a more flexible use of the interior. A wall that rises following a mechanism similar to a garage door has been installed in this apartment. The bedroom is open and the partition disappears into the ceiling.

0067 To avoid visually reducing the space of this bedroom and thus generating a continuum, doors that do not reach the floor or ceiling have been installed in the dressing area.

0068 A simple curtain separates the bedroom from the living room. Such partitions are very useful in small spaces. To emphasize the visual separation the bed has been placed on a white lacquered platform, which separates it from the rest of the apartment.

0069 An ensuite bathroom with a traditional layout can be transformed into an original space if the opaque partition walls are replaced with glass partitions. Transparency transforms and unifies the space and increases its luminosity.

0070 The centerpiece of this bathroom, which gives this project a unique quality, is a partition beside the wash-hand basin that separates the bathroom in two. This type of element, in addition to being a functional item gives identity to the space.

0071 This home, which has an irregular and experimental distribution, has lightweight and unobtrusive partitions, because there was no need to separate the different bedrooms.

0072 This bedroom has the bathroom integrated into the same space, but instead of screens, a glass partition has been installed separating the two areas. This choice protects the bedroom from excess moisture without breaking the visual continuity.

0073 The biggest advantage of partition walls is their versatility, their ability to adapt to almost any space. In this example, a built-in partition finished off with glass doubles up as a headboard and separates the bedroom and the shower area.

0074 Partitions, besides being major distribution elements of space, can form part of the decoration of the home and provide dramatic touches that add character to the home, as in this apartment by Studio Damilano.

0075 Translucent fiberglass panels, separate bedrooms and also create a relaxed atmosphere as they can filter the light passing through them.

0076 Almost all the walls of this home, with the exception of the street facing façades are made of glass. This is a good solution to let in maximum sunlight, particularly in areas with lower solar incidence such as Finland.

0074

0075

Floor plan

0076

0077

0078

0079

0080

0081

0082

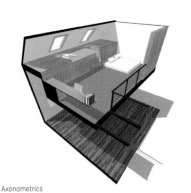

Axonometrics

0077 This original partition separates the bedroom from the living room. It consists of panels that open like an accordion and in the center, a semi-transparent panel with a built-in TV that pivots on an axis so that it can be seen from the two rooms.

0078 A translucent structure closes the bedroom area of this industrial-style apartment. Using this type of partition is a good way to customize the interior and shun more conventional styles of decoration.

0079 Although the bedroom shares space with the rest of the home, limits that act as separators have been established: a platform that subtly elevates the bedroom and a white curtain that acts as a false wall.

0080 In this refurbishment project, two resources have been used to divide spaces without losing natural light: half partitions, such as railings and glass walls to close the bedroom.

0081 In the refurbishment of this apartment the kitchen has been separated with an original partition: in addition to building a curved partition wall that creates a smoother transition, part of the wall is glass, thus not breaking the continuity with the surrounding space.

0082 The challenge when designing this house was to maintain the open space, improve the connection with the lower levels, while still maintaining privacy when necessary. Mobile panels were the solution: they offer thermal and acoustic insulation when needed.

0083 The double height of this home was created by making good use of the design of the roof of the house, which becomes gradually higher. This solution can increase the spaciousness in common areas like the dining room without losing useful floor space.

0084 If you have enough space and suitable height, high ceilings are a good solution to give more life to living rooms, which are the most popular areas of the house.

0085 Due to the irregular cuts in the lower floor and the extensive use of transparent glass the second level of the duplex opens onto some areas of the lower floor.

0086 One solution to prevent breaking the visual continuity in a room with double height like this one is to maintain the sleek design and include transparent elements, like the glass in the mezzanine railing.

0087 In this home, the kitchen has been installed in a double-height space. To close off the upper space, a semi-transparent material has been used, which contributes to the illumination of this working area.

0088 The double height of this living room has been used to install skylights instead of closing the space. This resource, which allows the interiors to have increased luminosity and comfort, is especially valuable when used in living areas.

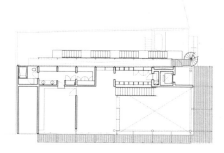

Floor plan

0086

▽

0087

0088

▽

0089

4F

Floor plans

5F

0090

0091

0092

0093

0094

0089 The two floors of this minimalist duplex are joined by two stairways at both ends of the apartment. This creates a double height area right in the living room area, increasing the sense of spaciousness.

0090 This home has made good use of the double height to install a wood stove; it is a good solution for energy efficiency, as a single heat source heats more rooms.

0091 This former sculpture workshop has become a large industrial-style loft. To achieve this, the height of the spaces has been expressly enhanced, as the rule-book says for this type of housing.

0092 The studio of Putney House is an open and light space. A small mezzanine has been installed taking advantage of the double height created by the slope of the roof. By not closing the upper level spatial continuity is created and the heat provided by wood stove is used.

0093 To take full advantage of the double heights in an interior, each space should be properly located. In this living room, for example, the dining area is located next to the kitchen, where a lot of space is not necessary.

0094 A good idea to connect the different levels is to install glass walls or large openings that show off the entire height.

0095 This bedroom has a wash-hand basin and a shower. To differentiate the spaces without adding doors or erecting walls, the level of the shower has been elevated, which is accessed through a built-in staircase.

0096 A simple painter's ladder or loft ladder is enough to access the top level. They are less bulky; thereby they do not occupy useful space. This item allows you to make the best use of a space and gain floor space in the home.

0097 Thanks to the accordion mechanism of these metal panels the spaces are more flexible without taking up too much space and they can separate the rooms according to whatever you need at that moment.

0095

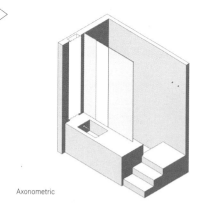

Axonometric

0096

0097

Floor plan

0098

0099

0100

0101

0098 The steps work here as an entrance to a space used as an office or study. Using the same material for the floor covering and the presence of a desk suggest continuity in spaces despite the difference in heights.

0099 A double height home is ideal for creating a new space. The mezzanines maximize space and light is not lost on either of the two levels.

0100 One option to visually connect the different levels is to install a glass railing. This element also provides increased security.

0101 In homes spread over many smaller floors, it can be interesting to design open levels that facilitates connection between the different spaces. This also creates the idea of visual spaciousness.

0102 A good organization of spaces in two-storey houses is to separate the rooms in terms of the privacy that each requires. In this case, it was not considered necessary to build walls to close the bedroom or study.

0103 A connection element such as a staircase can become a centerpiece give the interior personality, so it is important to choose wisely. In this case, an elegant staircase that combines wood and glass steps, allowing visual connection between levels.

0104 To make the interior space more flexible, build various levels, such as this triplex in New York. This option allows each room to have its own area without having to erect walls and constrain the space.

Floor plans

0105

0106

0107

0108

Sketch

0109

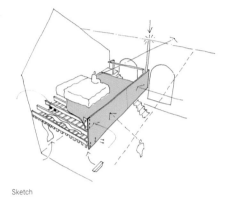

0105 To break the monotony of a uniform space, make use of different levels and gaps. In this home, small sofas and a table make use of a space buried into the floor.

0106 When designing a home, sometimes small intermediate levels are created. A good idea to use these often under-utilized spaces is to convert them into a reading corner or a small study.

0107 An open plan design is the best solution when designing double heights. This way it is possible to connect the different areas and heights with simple items such as pathways or large windows in the rooms on the top level.

0108 The combination of the materials in the mezzanine, plywood panels and untreated mild steel stairs, is the focal point of this structural element.

0109 To further visually lighten the space and provide good illumination when building a mezzanine floor, transparent materials can be used, as in this case, where glass has been used for mezzanine.

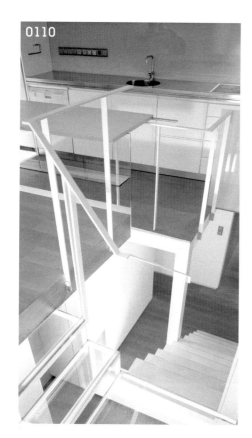

0110

0111

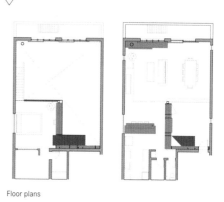

Floor plans

0112

0113

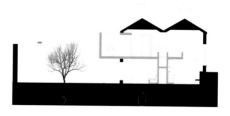

Cross section

0114

0115

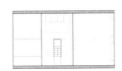

Floor plans

0116

Longitudinal section

0110 In the refurbishment of this dark attic a level was added to make use of the height of space. This solution also incorporates a lightweight glass and metal staircase allowing light to reach the lower level.

0111 In this loft in San Francisco the bedroom has been located on the top level. This solution does not affect the typical open-plan of this type of apartments but can separate the rooms in the home.

0112 These upper rooms may be left open to the rest of the home through a railing or building a half wall that allows, in turn, natural light to flood both levels.

0113 The refurbishment of this house included building a central polycarbonate volume with a mezzanine where the bedroom, dressing room and study were located. The floor plan is completely irregular as the two levels are not completely separated thus permitting interaction between public and private spaces.

0114 In large apartments, several points of access to different spaces and levels facilitate movement. In this loft in Madrid, several metal staircases have been installed for this purpose.

0115 Several levels have been created thanks to the height of this apartment: this was the only solution to maximize space and increase the usable surface area.

0116 The way the levels in a project are organized can define the final result. In this case, by taking advantage of the height of the apartment, an elevated level has been built that is defined by the sloping roof.

0117 Additional levels has been the solution used in this home, which is only 3 m (10 ft) wide, to avail of all rooms without losing surface or without having to build walls.

0118 A few steps separate the dining area and kitchen in the entrance to the house, creating a subtle division and a transition area between spaces that only changes in level and the combination of materials can create.

0119 This small space has been taken advantage of to position a desk. The use of levels to place rooms or areas is one of the best options for a distribution without walls or partitions.

0120 Leaving the metal structure that links the levels of the house exposed creates a contemporary and industrial look.

0121 The glass wall that closes off the bathroom is a good choice to highlight the height of the apartment. This transparency is what accentuates the presence of levels inside the home.

0122 The separation of spaces at different levels is a practical resource to organize uses and differentiate them even if they are in the same space. This small space is a studio/study with a view high above the rest of the apartment.

0123 The construction of a mezzanine floor in this apartment allows tenants to enjoy the magnificent views of the skyscrapers of the city of Chicago; from the top floor you can see the John Hancock Tower.

0124 Furniture can serve several functions within a space. In this case, the height of the wooden bookcase creates a partition that separates the living room and the attic, where the office is located.

0117

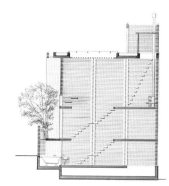

Longitudinal section

0118

0119

0120

0121

0122

0123

0124

0125

0126

0127

▽

0128

▷

0125 The change of material on a staircase defines the transition between levels: concrete for the first floor and living area and wood for the top floor where the bedrooms are located.

0126 The choice of staircase can change the perception of the interior. This spiral staircase occupies a limited space in the living room and the cables that surround it provide the necessary security and give it a lighter appearance.

0127 The architectural elements of the interiors, such as staircases, mezzanines or passages, must adapt to the available area of the house. In this case, a large staircase was changed for a large light and small spiral staircase.

0128 A staircase can change the perception of an interior. A simple stainless steel staircase and the neon lights in the shelves create a modern, youthful atmosphere in a luxurious modern apartment with more than 1000 m² (10,763 ft²).

0129 The stairs in this home are unique: they do not generate circulation through different areas of the house, but create back and forth movements, as each of them accesses a different room.

0130 A slate surface on a wall around the staircase, which is a busy transit zone, is an original and useful idea: creating an area for adults to leave notes and a space for children to draw.

0131 The black varnished iron staircase in Camilla Benedini's project is positioned near a window. The choice of this fine structure can connect different levels without relinquishing the natural light entering through the adjacent window.

0132 Staircases can also double up as additional storage space. In this duplex apartment the staircase is integrated into the space and contains extra closet space.

0133 One solution for small spaces with different levels is to organize the rooms around a central element, like a chimney, and include the staircase in this space. The result is both original and integrative.

0131

0132

0133

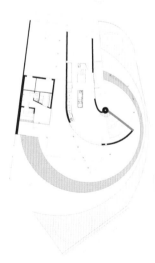

Floor plan

0134

0136

0135

0137

0134 To cause minimal disruption to the connection of the spaces, a reinforced glass handrail has been fitted to the staircase on the first floor of the house. This gives it a lightweight appearance that meets the idea of sought-after continuity.

0135 Architects must ensure that lighting in staircases is adequate and secure enough. The staircase leading to the suite on the top floor is lit by a side window and a low light that illuminates the steps at night.

0136 In small apartments it is important to take care over the design of the staircases that connect the different levels. Besides being connecting elements, they have such prominence in the interior that they become almost sculptural pieces.

0137 The materials used to construct the staircase can convert a passageway into a distinctive element in the home. The wood used in this staircase generates warmth and is perceived as an independent element.

0138 The eaves of the roof and elevated steps of this Canadian home protect the entrance of the house. This is one of the advantages of elevating steps in cold areas: they facilitate access in adverse weather conditions and heavy snow.

0139 A metal and glass staircase has been chosen to join the two levels of this house in Victoria, Australia. The size of the passages may limit the choice of connection type, although in this case the large space has not posed any problems.

0140 The staircase in this home by the architects Bricault Design is one of the elements that have been installed to create natural ventilation in the building. In addition to this environmental solution, the sculptural design of the staircase defines the aesthetic of the house.

0141 The perforated steel staircase leading to the mezzanine of this studio creates an industrial aesthetic, favoring an overall lighter perception and giving the apartment personality.

0142 The metal spiral staircase connects the different levels of the house, and is surrounded by a wooden cylinder in the children's bedrooms. In the kitchen it does not have a handrail. The lightness of the material means that it does not visually clutter the room.

0143 The lightweight folding steel ladder leading to the attic takes up minimal space and separates the lounge from the living room. In addition, it is a sculptural and decorative element in the home.

0144 Spiral staircases occupy less space than other types of staircases within a home. This idea is not at odds with the elegance and good design.

0141

0142

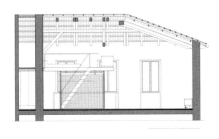

Longitudinal section

0143

0144

0145

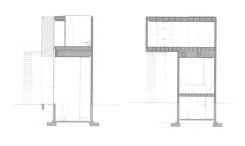

Sections

0146

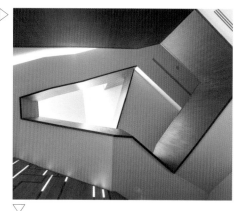

0147

0148

3D Representation

0149

0150

0145 This home is accessed via an external steel staircase that opens onto a small balcony that opens onto a public area. This element gives the home a unique feature.

0146 Staircases are connection elements which are particularly important in large homes. They separate public and private areas and generally have a high design factor that defines the decorative style of the house.

0147 The choice of the material for the stairs and other architectural elements can define the aesthetics of the interior. In this case, the central beam supports the wooden steps and makes them float and seem lighter.

0148 In this refurbishment by Anabela Leitão and Daiji Kondo, from A-LDK, a platform and a metal staircase have been installed giving access to the roof from the new master bedroom. By installing a lightweight metal structure a small terrace is created.

0149 An exterior staircase, located in a central courtyard of this Japanese home, has two objectives: to connect the two levels of the home and to not occupy floor space inside.

0150 Folding stairs are a good way to join levels: they take up little space and can easily be stored out of view. However they are more suitable for attics or spaces that are not used too often as bringing down or folding up the stairs may be a nuisance.

0151 The intermediate level of this impressive loft was mainly removed and an elegant walkway was created connecting the rooms located at both ends of the apartment as if it were a bridge over a river.

0152 The ramp is a good solution to provide a connection between the interior and exterior, which can be accessed by everyone, but unfortunately it is an option rarely used in residential interiors. KMW Promes Architects have made this a key element in the design of this house.

0153 There are a wide variety of entrances to homes but you must anticipate the needs for a rational design of the accesses. In this case a ramp, built so that vehicles can enter the estate, complements the staircase that crosses the divide.

0154 The uneven terrain has been used in the design of the space distribution of this home. The main body rests on the highest points and the ramp accessing the garage passes below, so as to avoid the composition and layout of the home.

0155 This elegant home is accessed via a walkway located over a pond, which brings distinction and defines the movement between the exterior and interior spaces.

0156 The Twin Project House by Uda presents a unique walkway that gives entry to the house through the roof. The existence of several entries provides easier access to the home, as the houses are built on sloping land, improving the circulation between the interior and exterior.

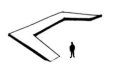

Design of the ramps

0154

0155

0156

Site plan

0157

0158

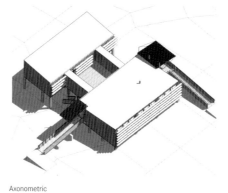

Axonometric

0159

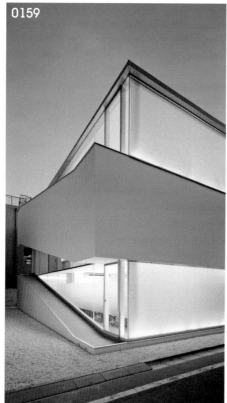

Floor plan

0160

0161

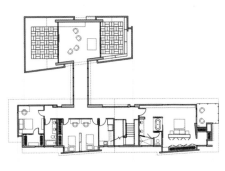

Floor plan

0157 This home stands on stilts to avoid altering the uneven terrains of the land and therefore it can be accessed made through a staircase and two walkways.

0158 The connections between the different levels of exterior terraces have been achieved through a unique combination of steps and a simple wooden walkway leading to the lagoon pier. The levels are unified with the use of the same wood.

0159 The ramp that surrounds the house has gently unified all levels of the house without interfering with the interior, from the office to the private rooms.

0160 Walkways are a good choice to join pavilions when they are spread over a lot. In this example, they also serve to connect spaces that were built on pillars and minimize the impact on the land.

0161 This closed walkway connects the two wings of the first floor of a home in San Diego. The glass walls allow light to enter and let you see the garden, which creates a dynamic link and original element in the design of the house.

0162 A walkway that can be raised and lowered as if it were the bridge of a castle is used to connect the main body of the house to the volume that contains the indoor pool, over which a terrace has been built.

0163 Connections between the interior and exterior can be created visually. Stone slabs laid on the gravel undoubtedly mark the driveway to the home. On this occasion, the visual difference of the stone, gravel and slab defines the boundaries of the spaces.

0164 Ramps are elements that connect different levels and offer better accessibility than stairs, especially for people with reduced mobility. Their inclusion in the design of a home can give the construction added value.

0165

0166

0167

0168

0165 By using the glass on the walls of this home in Paradise Valley, Arizona, a bright and clear corridor has been created. This solution also allows the visual connection with the exterior areas of the house.

0166 To differentiate spaces decorate them in completely different styles. The reception area/hall of this New York apartment stands out for the circle-patterned wallpaper and the eye-catching black vinyl floor.

0167 If the corridors are wider than standard, closets or bookcases can be fitted that increase the storage space of the house. In this apartment sliding door cabinets stand out.

0168 The housing program, the glass expanses in the corridor area and the staircase of the top floor follow the instructions of the architect and manage to create a sense of spatial freedom.

0169 Translucent material has been used to give the corridor in this home light. This solution reduces the use of artificial lighting while maintaining a certain degree of privacy in the interior.

0170 Large homes tend to have passages or spaces that connect the rooms. This stylish hall connects the dressing room with the master bedroom.

0171 The location of the corridor at one end of the rectangular house makes the opposite facade fully visible. Thus, none of the rooms are interrupted and you can enjoy the view from each of them.

0172 Connecting spaces should be designed taking into account the lighting that they will receive both at day and night. In this case, the large windows and a wall of glass allow the corridor on the second floor to be lit up with natural light during the day.

0173 When the goal is to create a clean and fresh ambience, choose materials that reinforce this decoration, such as polished cement floors and walls painted white.

0174 In this Japanese-inspired home the living area is separated from the bedrooms. The spaces are joined by an evocative glass corridor that allows you to view the exterior garden and also does not interrupt the visual connection.

0175 The corridor leading from the lounge to the bedrooms was created with a large wooden bookcase extending from floor to ceiling. Using furniture to create or enhance connections in a home fuses architecture and decoration.

0176 The decoration on the walls, such as this black and white image of a forest, makes the interior spaces more dynamic and in this case is the connection between the corridor and the living room.

0169

0170

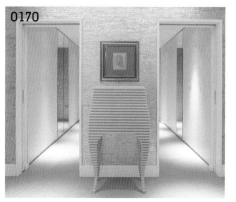

0171

0172

0173

0174 ▷

◁

Floor plan

0175 ▷

0176 ▷

0177 A pivoting closet that serves as a wall is the centerpiece of this apartment. The closet can be moved to increase the surface area of the studio or living room, as appropriate.

0178 An ottoman bed is one of the clearest examples of how the furniture can be transformed and helps to organize a home. Although sometimes the change is imperceptible, as in this case, in which the bed is concealed in a small closet.

0179 A simple shelf in the TV unit converts this space into a small studio: creativity prevails over costly solutions.

0180 A folding table provides additional work space when needed without reducing natural light. When folded it fits into the studio and appears to be part of the wall.

0177

0178

0179

0180

0181

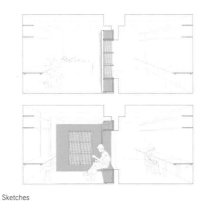

Sketches

0182

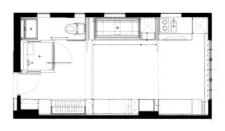

Floor plan

0183

0181 Reflecting on the use of space and the role of furniture can achieve hybrid solutions that improve the use of the rooms. This moving wall increases the space available in the studio by taking advantage of the bedroom that is not used during the day.

0182 Solutions based on mobile and transformable furniture allow maximum utilization of space: rails on the roof are used to slide a piece of furniture that hides the kitchen area in this small apartment.

0183 A sofa bed is perhaps the most versatile convertible furniture and most successful of all those that exist. It can be used daily in small houses or sporadically and it always serves a dual role.

0184 Sometimes it is not necessary to have certain areas due to the lack of a specific place to locate them. The same room can have several functions using convertible furniture, such as in the Switch project by Yuko Shibata, where the dining room and office share the same space.

0185 The installation of transformable furniture configures a studio in accordance with the lifestyle of the owner and allows for the simultaneous use of rooms such as the kitchen and dining room or bedroom and bathroom.

0186 The intelligent use of space adds value to the design of Carter + Burton Architecture. This spacious room, where yoga classes are given, also serves as a living room and kitchen. In addition, it conceals beds in the floor.

0187 Installing a folding bed is the perfect solution to transform a studio or a second living room into a temporary guest bedroom: they take up little space and allows a more flexible use of the room.

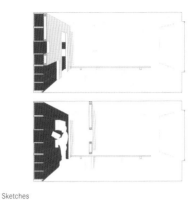

Sketches

0188

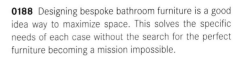

0189

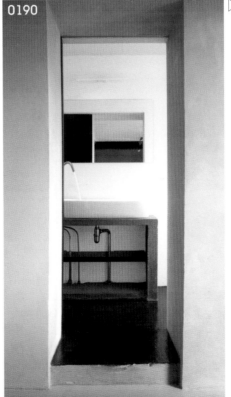

0190

0191

0188 Designing bespoke bathroom furniture is a good idea way to maximize space. This solves the specific needs of each case without the search for the perfect furniture becoming a mission impossible.

0189 In the refurbishment of the house in California a built-in bathtub was constructed. The materials used some simple earth-tone tiles, unify the space even though a glass wall separates the bath and shower area from the rest of the room.

0190 In this small bathroom concrete was used to construct the sink unit, which adds strength to the space and creates an industrial aesthetic.

0191 The main advantage of built-in furniture is that it adapts to any application: this vanity unit has its own unique features such as the pivoting mirrors and concealed shelves that can be used as bedside tables.

0192 Warm colors and materials with a simple design are the solutions to visually unite the kitchen closets with the living room in this English home. The dining table and bench, which also doubles up as storage, follow the same principles.

0193 Built-in furniture and the use of the color white have created a spacious kitchen that is integrated into the circulation spaces of the apartment: at one end some compact closets and at the other a more light-weight and illuminated work island.

0194 The kitchen is organized around an island that manages to integrate the living and dining room. The chosen furniture and built-in shelves create a cozy environment more suited to a living room than a contemporary kitchen.

0195 The kitchen of this home is built around a fire-place, which is the centerpiece of the room. The furniture is fully integrated into this room and is enhanced by the lighting embedded into the closets of the kitchen bench.

Floor plan

0196 Spaces can be unified stylistically thanks to the furnishings. Using the same wood in the kitchen and living room furniture of this Australian home creates a wide space in which there are no clear boundaries between one function and another.

0197 The use of cheaper materials like concrete in some areas of the house, for example the kitchen, reduces the budget and provides a simpler design of the spaces.

0198 There are no closets in this kitchen, for work surfaces concrete has been used, which is also present on the floors and walls, and stainless steel shelves have been installed for storage.

0199 Furniture that creates separations in a single room has been used in the design of this home in Norway. For example, the kitchen is integrated into the central space of the first floor and the use of wood throughout the interior aesthetically links it with the rest of the house.

0200 The dark wood used for furniture and kitchen cladding covers the walls and defines the visual boundaries that separate it from the living room. The furniture design creates an open space that connects the two areas.

0201 To integrate the kitchen into an open space it is recommended to use built-in furniture, at least in part. Using the same materials in several areas, such as wood or concrete beams, unifies the style.

0202 Social changes are reflected in the design of furniture. They manage to promote the coexistence of rooms in the same space. This kitchen, for example, can be easily transformed into a dining room due to the integration of the island-style table.

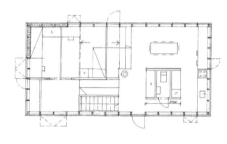

Floor plan

0203

0204

0205

0206

Detail of the shelves

0203 Resistant curtains can be a practical and economical solution to close the storage space, such as in this apartment in Warsaw.

0204 Shelves can be customized to suit the decorative tastes of the owners. A colored shelving system fills the entire length of the wall in this bright study.

0205 The width of the hall on the first floor has meant a few bookcases can be installed storing the owner's extensive book collection.

0206 Built-in book shelves visually lighten the wall and create a dynamic passage and integrated with the bookcase. A sliding panel closes the passage leaving one of the bookcases outside, which can be used by both rooms.

0207 To maximize storage space in this house, the closets were built with prefabricated modules and positioned along the side walls.

0208 The potential storage furniture in a kitchen is almost endless: work surfaces, appliances, etc. Study the needs to find the best solution.

0209 Integrating the shelves on the wall of the study or library instead of installing furnishings contributes to consolidating the decorative style of the room and visually lightening the space.

0210 Built-in furniture is the best solution when you have it very clear how to organize the spaces of a home. This does not exclude the possibility of using other furniture that can change location.

0211 Finnish wooden mobile panels can expose or conceal storage with built-in shelving. The system provides flexibility in storage space and prevents monotony in the room.

0212 Corridors are ideal places to place closets, mezzanines, racks or any other storage element. In this New York loft, a wooden piece of furniture defines the corridor, distributes the rooms and contains closets.

0210

0211

0212

0213 Bespoke furniture makes interiors more flexible and more dynamic spaces. Bespoke design changes the usual concept of interiors: it is not the owner who adapts to the space, but the space that accommodates the needs of the inhabitants.

0214 The pinpoint distribution of the furniture is the distinguishing feature of this small apartment in Barcelona. The bespoke furnishings are what define the use of the only room at all times: bedroom, living room, kitchen, study.

0215 These custom made set of shelves make use of a space next to a staircase and become a corner with two functions: decoration and storage.

0216 A white lacquered unit covers the whole wall of the living room. This solution combines two concepts that sometimes seem incompatible: large capacity and low visual impact.

0213

0214

0216

Floor plan

0215

0217

Floor plan

0218

0219

0220

0217 This bedroom has one piece of furniture that combines the structure of the bed, desk and chair. The physical continuity of the distribution of different corners is the hallmark of the room.

0218 One of the walls of this home in London has specially designed closets for this room and shelves that flank the plasma screen.

0219 Bespoke furniture adapts to any space and any type of object. In this home, closets have been specifically built to store surfboards.

0220 The solution for the beds and closets in the nursery: custom designed furniture to position in an enclave, saving a lot of space.

0221 Closets can become part of the aesthetic character of the house; these lacquered volumes located next to the living room provide storage space while creating a plastic effect of light and shadow.

0222 When bespoke furniture is designed, other features can be added to complement its main use as a storage space. In this case, the bookcase in this home also serves as a partition that separates the study from the living room.

0223 The maintenance of exterior furniture is something to consider in a second home. This is non-existent when the furniture is built-in: on this terrace a concrete exterior table the base for the sofas has been built.

0224 The bed of this small studio is hidden to make more space in the central area during the day. The headboard has a few small shelves built-in.

0225

0226

Floor plan

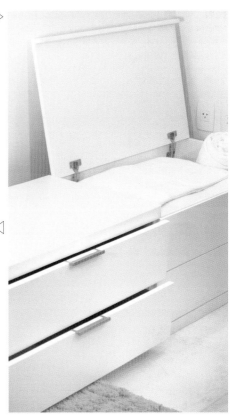

0227

0228

0225 Take full advantage of high ceilings and double heights to gain more storage space with attics or closets. In this London home, for example, closets have been installed in some areas of the home with double height.

0226 Low units usually contain drawers or doors that open at the front. The top chest-type opening is the perfect solution when the size of the apartment and the positioning of the furniture make access more difficult.

0227 Playing with the resources that create the materials is one of the best options for customizing the interior of the house. The materials used in kitchen furniture, for example, can mimic it with the environment or mark a contrast to reaffirm its presence.

0228 The priority for natural lighting restricts the possibilities of the furniture in the living room. A low unit next to the large window that continues the minimalist style of the decoration is a bookcase and stores the stereo.

0229 A unit has been fitted that has a dual function in the guest bedroom: storage when closed and a desktop when opened. The transformation of the space is due to this single detail.

0230 The positioning of closets and storage spaces should not be last minute decisions in interior design. In this case, the owners requested multiple storage spaces and designed a linear closet in the kitchen area.

0231 When a lack of space is a problem, a bespoke closet may be the solution however it can be expensive, although it takes advantage of tight corners, badly-located columns, etc. and rearranges the layout of the house.

0232 Children's rooms, which are generally smaller in size, should have enough space to store games, books, school material and also have play area. Bespoke furniture allows you to customize the rooms and resolve these needs.

0233 The shelves behind the sofa are arranged diagonally, thus providing space to store books without having to take away width from the passageway.

0234 The combination of high and low closets and the use of the same design and color in the living room and kitchen furniture was the right decision: the storage space was increased without altering the minimalist aesthetic of the house.

0235 Any corner or any uneven wall can accommodate storage space if the furniture is designed properly. In this room, closets and drawers are located on the side and the lower part of an original sofa.

0236 The hybrid furniture, sofa and set of shelves in a single volume, personalize interiors and add value to designs that are complemented with other pieces by the same creators.

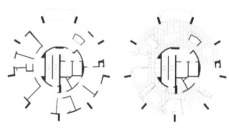

Floor plans

0232

0233

0234

0235

0236

0237 The irregularity of the shelves and different widths of the columns are the keys to give a more dynamic and youthful style to a classic storage furniture such as a bookcase.

0238 Wooden soffits integrated into the floor conceal spaces like the bathroom or bedroom. This is possible thanks to the design of a specific furniture unit for this house.

0239 In the living room and the studio of this home, located at different levels, the same gray storage furniture has been used to achieve a stylish unity in all environments.

0240 To achieve a spacious room, suitable for social gatherings, without losing storage space, a bespoke unit has been designed with sliding doors and the use of wood has been unified.

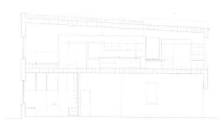

Longitudinal section

0241

0242

0243

Floor plan

0244

0241 By placing shelves along the wall the entire perimeter of the living room that also doubles up as a study is used. The backdrop of the shelves has been customized according to needs.

0242 The bookcase and shelves are located under the mezzanine. They have been designed and constructed in light colors and lightweight materials so as to not visually clutter the room that has a dual-use: living room and study.

0243 The staircase has many functions within the house thanks to its integrated and unique design: the partition that separates the living room from the kitchen and it provides storage space. In addition, it is perceived as a piece of furniture through the use of wood.

0244 The use of the wall that encloses the staircases to fit a few shelves is a very practical solution, especially when the hall or the room is wide enough.

0245

0246

0247

0248

0249

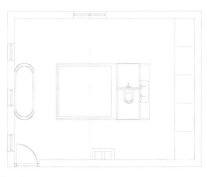

Floor plan

0250

0251

0252

0245 This ingenious cube was designed to accommodate the bedroom, shelves and storage space, a full wardrobe on one side and a bed for two dogs.

0246 The bedroom is located in a compact plywood unit. On one side and the base are the cabinets and some small drawers that provide extra storage space.

0247 This module designed by i29 unifies the so-called water area. The interior space of the unit contains the bathtub while the kitchen has been integrated into the exterior. These modules speed up construction because installation is faster.

0248 The kitchen and bathroom of this apartment are in the same space, which also differs from the rest of the house owing to its use of wood. This kind of module brings together the water and gas pipes in the same space and thus facilitates the installation of these supplies.

0249 Compact modules can make full use of space in smaller rooms. In this 35 m² (376ft²) space, a module has been installed that combines the toilet, shower, wash-hand basin and bed, which reduces the space that would be needed if a bedroom with a conventional bathroom was built.

0250 In this bedroom, a unit encompassing the bed and the bathroom has been built. The very original design fits the decor of the apartment. This odd choice that stylistically unifies the spaces, works especially well in small sized houses or lofts.

0251 When the doors of this module are closed they form a compact element, but when opened reveal a large capacity for storage and order.

0252 To preserve the openness of the apartment, all useful functions are centralized in a single block containing a kitchenette, a toilet, a shower and a bathtub.

0253 In this refurbishment, an interior polycarbonate-covered structure has been built. Polycarbonate is a lightweight, highly resistant material that is gaining ground for its use in architecture. When translucent, as in this case, it creates lighting effects.

0254 Materials can define the character of the house. The rough surface of concrete applied to interior walls contrasts sharply with the smoothness and refinement of other materials used, such as floor tiles or stone and bathroom wall tiles.

0255 Tatami mats, typically made from straw, are associated with Japanese traditions, such as the tea ceremony. It is now reserved for these ceremonies or special rooms. The dimensions and placement are subject to certain rules.

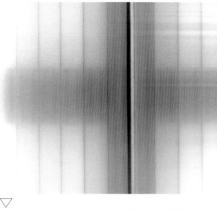

0256

0257

0258

0259

0256 If you want to define each of the functions without dividing them, it is possible to do so visually, through elements such as flooring, walls and ceiling. By changing the floor covering material, or just changing the color and texture, you can define each zone.

0257 Wood is one of the most used materials for floors, especially in interiors seeking a warm and comfortable aesthetic. A certified wooden floor has been laid in this space, designed by Carter + Burton Architecture, which is also used as a yoga center.

0258 Inside this Swiss home, the uncoated/unfinished stone walls have been maintained. The use of this material provides a rustic look to the entire house and the exposed texture that makes it unnecessary to add any other ornaments.

0259 An original material for use in domestic floors is concrete, economic and quick to be applied. The finish may be more or less polished in terms of the style you want to give the home, either industrial or sensitive.

0260 The fabric from the Botanic range of the Norwegian company Bolon, reflects the richness of the plant world. Representations of vinyl flowers, herbs and plants are inspired by images of nature. The palette of earth tones is combined with bright touches of yellow and green.

0261 The use of different materials will help to break the continuity of the floor covering and create a more dynamic interior. In this case, metallic sheets, with their texture and form, are an innuendo to the optical illusions of reversibility of the drawings by M. C. Escher.

0262 Stoneware tiles, in their different compositions, are the most common solution for floor covering in kitchens and bathrooms. This material is tough and there is a wide variety of finishes offered by commercial companies to suit all owners' tastes.

0263 When the color palette is mainly neutral tones, breaks the monotony of the walls by applying wallpapers with volume and superimposed graphics. In this case, the importance of these resources can be seen in the interior finish of this home.

0260

0261

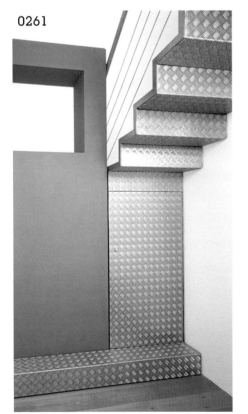

0262

0263

0264 Inside a polycarbonate wall has been erected to surround the staircase. This material, besides being a visual design element, allows the light to pass through the interior of the house, thereby reducing the need for artificial lighting.

0265 The industrial aesthetic of this loft has been achieved through the use of a bright red synthetic floor. Using this type of plastic material, which is very strong and comes in varied textures, is becoming increasingly common in the interiors of homes.

0266 Tropical woods like ipe, mahogany, teak and ca-maru are very resistant to moisture, making them most suitable for the flooring in the bathroom or kitchen.

0267 The walls and floor of the bathroom are covered with white and gray tiles. This material is very suitable for wet areas like bathrooms, kitchens and swimming pools for its insulating and waterproof capacity.

0268 Ipe wood has been used for the floor of the porch of this home. This wood is very dense and has very good natural durability. Over time, when exposed to UV rays and weathering, it acquires a more uniform and grayish color.

0269 The choice of material has been given prominence in this kitchen. In this case, bamboo, found in floors, walls and ceiling, has been chosen which includes the space in a single volume.

0270 In the exterior parts of the manufactured home a metallic grid has been installed as a floor covering. This material, besides being low cost, is easy to maintain, and particularly suitable for areas with extreme climates.

0286

▽

0287

0288

0289

▽

▷

0290 Maintaining the original floor, if it is well preserved, is an option to consider when refurbishing a home. In many cases, the character of the architecture can be maintained and creates an interior with more personality.

0291 In the bathroom of the master bedroom of this prefabricated home, tiles have been laid only in the bathtub area, which has more direct contact with water. The rest of the room has been finished with a traditional white paint.

0292 An appropriate decision to emphasize the continuity of the spaces in these loft-style apartments is the use of a solid floor, as in this apartment in Seattle, where black, polished concrete has been chosen for the floor covering.

0293 In the bathroom of the project by Makoto Tamaguchi a mirrored wall has been fitted instead of hanging the traditional framed mirror in front of the wash-hand basin. This original idea increases the feeling of spaciousness of a room, visually doubling its surface area.

0295

0296

0297

0294 In bathrooms and kitchens it is normal to lay a more resistant flooring. In this room, for example, the finish of the flooring can be fully appreciated, different depending on whether it is the bathroom or bedroom area.

0295 To create a warm atmosphere in the children's bedroom of the apartment in Hong Kong, fabric was used to line the walls and carpet on the floor. The palette of colors, mostly neutral, reinforces this final ambience.

0296 The original terracotta tile floor of this Paris apartment has been restored. On occasions this solution is not the cheapest, but it is definitely the one that best maintains the original character of the buildings.

0297 The combination of ceramic materials and stone favors a dynamic interior, especially when using different sizes, colors and textures. This bathroom, for example, combines large brown slabs with white tile.

0298 Concrete was the material chosen for the floor of this apartment. To diffuse the harshness of its texture and color and remove the industrial references, a warm dark red paint was chosen.

0299 Prefabricated materials and those of certified provenance are the best choice to shorten construction times. The quality, as can be seen on the floor and walls of this home, is the same as conventional materials.

0300 Marble is a traditional material, but the finishes can transform a classic a prioiri bathroom into a contemporary room. In this case, an original glass opening in the wall of the shower modifies the perception of this space.

0298

0299

0300

0301

0302

0303

0304

0301 Slightly raising the floor of the kitchen and bathroom, both water areas, is very common when the location of these rooms is changed. It's an easy way to solve the problem of installing drains and pipes.

0302 The option of using pure white for the floors and walls provides clarity and width to the rooms. This is necessary if you want to choose darker-colored furniture as is the case of this home in Hong Kong.

0303 The contrast between the wooden and ceramic finish means that walls or doors are not necessary to define this space. In interiors with open spaces the combination of materials is a good solution to define the use given to each surface.

0304 The light brown marble floor covering in the entrance and the apartment study creates a sophisticated and elegant ambience. This material is also extremely durable.

0305 This roof has been designed with environmentally friendly materials. The roof is covered with vegetation helping to regulate the temperature inside the house, while the ceiling has been built with layers of bamboo, a natural and recyclable material.

0306 Concrete is one of the most used materials in architecture for the foundations, walls and floors. This project, which has left the concrete exposed in the ceiling, stands out for its simplicity in the use of materials.

0307 Using the same material in ceilings and walls is an option that serves two functions: reducing costs and creating a particular aesthetic in the house, especially in this case, in which small wooden slabs have been used.

0308 To prevent the interior design of a minimalist home becoming monotonous, play with the shapes of some of the elements. The undulating ceiling of this apartment brings dynamism and avoids excessive simplicity.

0309

0310

0311

0309 The use of synthetic materials is a good option to achieve unique effects. On the walls and the roof of the home, for example, a urethane resin varnish has been used in this case in greenish tones.

0310 The ceiling of the sustainable home designed by Zen Architects has been clad in wooden panels. The height of the ceilings and the combination with the white walls enhance the spaciousness of the rooms and provide warmth to the kitchen and dining room.

0311 The gambrel roof exposes the wood beams used in the construction of the new covering. By not installing a false ceiling there is more available space and the construction standards in the area have been complied with.

0312 The pitched roof is visible on the top floor of the home located in Naijing and reveals the concrete used to build both the ceiling and roof.

0313 Materials can change the perception of the spaces; part of this ceiling is covered with a mirrored surface that visually amplifies the size of the room.

0314 The roof and ceilings of this Californian home were built with steel. This material could be considered as sustainable, as most production is made from recycled cars.

0315 On the flat roof of the Chilean home, gravel and concrete slabs have been used so that it can be walked on. These materials are combined with skylights and shade to promote the use of this area.

0316 The roof of this home has been designed taking into account the changes of the main air currents and sun that the house receives. Thus, the roof extends onto the south façade, closing the house while the north side is more open.

0317 The new roof of this home is conglomerate but the finish includes other elements: several lamps and a skylight are interspersed in the wood to control the light that it receives in the interior.

0318 The unique form of the roof of this house is due to an initial requirement: rainwater had to be collected. The architects opted for this form and the use of slate to respond to the client's request.

0319 The roof of the extension of this London home has been built with aluminum, but to increase the lighting and fuse the boundaries with the exterior, it has been finished with glass.

0320 The essential characteristic of this home is its finish in the form of pools or ponds. These structures, which collect rainwater, partly solve the interior air conditioning of the house, necessary in this area of Turkey.

0321 The roofs of this apartment from the early twentieth century maintain the original elements and the light gray finish makes the plaster moldings stand out.

0322 Some architectural structures necessarily define the shape of the interior, such as the curvature of the wooden roof of the houseboat. The idea of maintaining the exterior curvature in the interior adds lightness to the whole space.

0319

0320

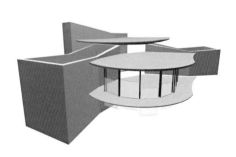

3D Representation

0321

0322

0323

0324

0325

0326

0323 Painting the walls and ceiling bright colors adds personality to the interior of the house. In this New York apartment the color black adds strength and contributes to the eclectic interior.

0324 The perception of the interiors can vary with a single detail in the finishes. This ceiling covered with floral green wallpaper adds a tone of luxury to the master bedroom.

0325 An overhanging roof is a common solution for providing shade and protection from inclement weather. In this case, the roof has been extended with a synthetic semitransparent material, which is easily replaceable and inexpensive.

0326 The combination of finishes in the interior of the home is used to highlight the spaces and use the right materials. The metallic finishes of this home line the floor, walls and ceiling in some areas.

0327 The doors to the terraces of this New York penthouse are glass with metalwork, some of which are double doors. These glass doors have improved the views of the Hudson River.

0328 This house has two double doors: an interior glass door and an exterior metal door. This solution serves to allow light to enter during the day without relinquishing security.

0329 Security and privacy are issues to consider, in this house in Arizona a large metal pivot door provides access to the garden and completes and closes the wall protecting the home.

0330 Aidlin Darling Design architects intended to fuse the boundaries between the interior and exterior of the home. To enhance this continuity glass doors have been used for the access doors and the same interior and exterior floor covering.

0331

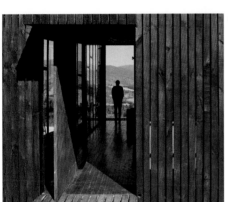

0332

0333

0331 Wood is the main feature of the entrance to this home. The door helps to provide a monolithic appearance to the home, as it is located on the west façade, which has wood paneling to preserve the privacy of the occupants.

0332 A large glass conservatory is a good solution to give character to the entrance of a single family home. Natural light and the transparency of the space enable visitors to find their bearings. This conservatory, located on the southeast façade, provides access to the two wings of the home.

0333 The house is surrounded by metal railings which includes two gateways, one for vehicles and another for pedestrians, which were included in the gate so that you can pass by unnoticed.

0334 Front doors allow a multitude of combinations in terms of form and material, and gives character to the homes. In this case, wood is combined with glass.

0335 Sometimes the original architectural structures such as doors, windows, moldings, etc need to be maintained when refurbishing a house. This apartment has retained the front door, which has been painted white to integrate it into the current space.

0336 Tall pivoting glass doors arranged in parallel are the solution to take advantage of air currents in the area and contribute to the cooling and ventilation of the house. Glass has been used to enjoy views of the valley.

0337 In this house located in Hiroshima large wooden doors with a bellowed opening have been installed that protect the entire façade from the weather, particularly typhoons.

0338

0339

0340

0342

0341

0338 To address the lack of space, integrated sliding doors have been installed that when open can be moved around the hallway and, if necessary, close the space and act as walls for various rooms, bathroom and bedroom.

0339 Exterior sliding doors are perfect to close small or narrow spaces, as you do not lose floor space.

0340 By using glass as the main material on the exterior walls of these lofts in Seattle, the architects have managed to dispel the differences between the architectural elements: windows, fixed panels and access doors to the balcony are unified.

0341 If the house has patios it is interesting to establish connection between the interior and exterior. In this case, for example, a large bellowed door opens the bathroom onto an interior courtyard and creates the perfect setting for a relaxing bath.

0342 There are many ways to clad interior doors, in this case, silver sheets cover the door and the wall of this home in Italy to add uniqueness to the interior.

0343 The steps leading from the hall to the studio have been lengthened to give continuity to the sliding door and integrate it into the space without creating a visual break. The choice of the same wood used in the walls creates this continuity.

0344 Sliding doors are perfectly integrated into the walls elegantly separating different areas without taking up space or interfering with the interior design of the rooms. In this apartment in Shanghai, for example, the dining room is closed with sliding glass doors.

0345 The glass doors that surround the living room of this home in California meet a very special function: they create the conditions for an open and flexible ambience, geared towards a lifestyle of living with the community.

0346 The large sliding glass doors connect the newly constructed area with the patio, and as they are installed on the south façade, they also allow maximum utilization of daylight hours.

0347

0348

0349

0350

0347 Sliding doors separate the living space from the study area in a subtle way. When pulled over they serve as the headboard of the living room couch and unite the two spaces.

0348 Sufficient quality in sliding glass doors ensures good climate control and a real comfort of the interiors. Tempered and laminated glass also provides security.

0349 A sliding door saves space. If rooms are small, as is the case of this extension, conventional doors limit circulation.

0350 A partial solution to separate the rooms in open apartments is to install sliding glass doors. They change the visual perception of the space and allow the tenants to isolate themselves from the noise when they need to concentrate.

0351 The combination of different types of windows and large windows can change the look of a house, the façade of this Australian home combines sliding doors and laminated windows to avoid monotony in the façade.

0352 The master bedroom on the first floor features a large corner window that occupies two of the walls of the room and also allows you to enjoy the lake view without any visual interruption.

0353 Urban apartments do not always face the correct direction to capture optimal sunlight. A good solution to take full advantage is to install double-height windows that light up the two levels of the home.

0354 Built for two graphic designers, this home in California stands between two redwood groves. The façade facing north has large windows from floor to ceiling to enjoy the light and the view of the mountain.

0355 The location of this home in a wooded area and the decision not to cut down any trees led the architects María Victoria Besonías, Guillermo de Almeida and Luciano Kruk of BAK architects, to build large windows that allow light to enter.

0356 The best solution to improve the natural lighting in homes is for the house to face south. In this house the south façade, with large windows and glass doors, contrasts with the opposite more closed and wooden façade.

0357 The typical viewpoint of many London houses can be used to locate multiple spaces and create varied environments: in this case, the white curtains have converted it into a minimalist dining room with ethereal lighting.

0358 The majority of the façades of the house are glazed to increase the presence of natural light. It is important that these large windows do not impede the circulation of both people and drafts. Thus, there are openings both on the first floor and on the second floor.

0351

0352

0353

0354

▷

0355

0356

▽

0357

0358

▷

0359 The windows stud the walls of this prefabricated home in Massachusetts. The option to install as many openings, both the upper and lower walls, provides the possibility of opening windows on all façades, which regulates the entry of air.

0360 The windows of this home are fixed, except for a small part that is operable. This was devised to create cross ventilation without losing security and lighting that the fixed windows provide.

0361 Corner windows allow more light and maximize views. In this case fixed windows have been installed in the office area but another smaller part of the window has been left operable to aid ventilation.

0362 To facilitate the lighting of the interiors and while avoiding the rigor of the sunlight, the window of this home in Los Angeles has been installed on the lower part of the wall.

0363 Horizontal pivoting windows, which in this case form part of a glass wall, are typical of industrial areas. The idea of keeping them in transformed spaces in houses contributes to a more authentic loft aesthetic.

0364 The windows in this home have insulated glass with low emissivity or low-e, which prevents heat from entering the house in summer and escaping in winter. They are opened at night to make the house cooler and are kept closed during the day.

0365 The wall of the bathroom located on the south side has large laminated windows. This type of window ventilates the room in a flexible way and allows you to enjoy the landscape without the need for large openings in the walls.

0366 The installation of blinds meets the necessary function to filter the light entering the house and suit the needs of each space, but it also manages to create interesting patterns of light throughout the day.

0367 The windows that cover one of the façades of the renovated apartment maintain their original aesthetic. Sheer curtains have been the solution to integrate them into the new décor of the house.

0368 Windowsills provide an additional space that can be used as a bench or shelf. In this room, it serves as an extension of the bedside table.

0369 Glass walls enhance their effectiveness if windows are installed in them that ventilate the interiors. In this loft designed by Kerry Joyce Associates the partial openings of the windows stand out.

0370 A suitable option for privacy is to install, either partially or completely, glazed windows, in the bedroom windows or rooms where you want more privacy.

0371 A good place to locate a studio or an office desk is in a corner near a window, as good lighting, preferably natural, is essential in these areas.

0367

Floor plans before and after

0368

0369

0371

0370

0372

0373

0374

0372 Windows installed on roofs perform several functions: they light up rooms that would otherwise be in darkness and ventilate these interiors. To prevent heat loss in winter these windows are double or triple glazed.

0373 After studying the air currents in the area, it was decided that the ideal place to install operable windows was in the lower part of the glass walls of this living room. Its function is to promote cross ventilation and avoid the use of air conditioning.

0374 Sash windows, like those in this room, are composed of one or more operable panes that move in a vertical direction on rails or guides. Their originality is that, when opened, the panes overlap.

0375

0376

Floor plan

0377

0378

0379

0380

0381

0382

0375 To bring light into the interior of the lower floors, which are darker than the top floors it is a good idea to install a skylight, either fixed or operable. It is important to consider the climate to decide on the degree of insulation that this element must provide.

0376 A large skylight closes a double-height space which connects the different rooms on the first floor. This solution allows light to reach the lower floors so as to not lose the quality of life. In this case, vegetation has been planted.

0377 In the living area of this home, the walls with skylights have been closed to increase the visibility of the interiors. Some of these skylights are operable, thereby generating cross ventilation that airs the rooms.

0378 In homes located in areas closer to the Poles, as is the case with this house in Iceland, light entry should be optimized to take advantage of the months with less sunshine. Skylights in the roof are a good solution for this problem.

0379 The geography and climate influence the design of a home. The large sloping skylight lets in more natural light in this Dutch home.

0380 A unique circular skylight has been opened between the first floor and basement, so that natural light vertically floods the home. The new fixed opening made from reinforced glass, does not reduce the usable area of the room.

0381 The entire perimeter of the house has multiple openings and glass walls, but it also has fixed skylights in the top part of the wall that increase the feeling of openness and transparency of the interior.

0382 The layout of the skylights in the room can define the lighting that it will receive. The bedroom, for example, enjoys indirect light that creates a relaxed atmosphere.

0383 Reforming a small space like a balcony and gaining a few square meters is a good idea, especially if the balcony has a view. In this case, as the balcony has breathtaking views of a park, it has been furnished with sofas and armchairs suitable for outdoor use.

0384 If an apartment is small, expand the square footage by using the space of the balcony or terrace. Here, a small lounge and dining room, both with outdoor furniture has been installed for easier maintenance.

0385 When the balcony views do not add value, the best option is to take this opportunity to turn it into an extension of the interior. The wood paneling and windows that separate the interior and exterior diffuse the boundaries between both.

0386 When the balcony is large, as is the case with this house in the Norwegian town of Strand, treat this space like a terrace and make the most of the outdoors space.

0387 To create dynamism in the façades, different types of openings (windows, glass walls, terraces and balconies) can be alternated, allowing a more direct connection with the environment.

0388 One of the best ways to achieve privacy in an urban environment is to plant hedges or shrubs that grow to a certain height. These textile blinds, as in this balcony in Barcelona, provides complete privacy.

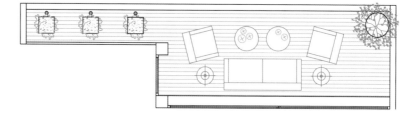

Balcony floor plan

0386

0387

0388

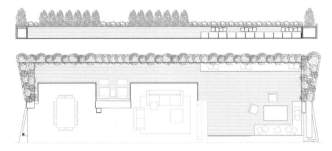

Elevation and balcony floor plan

0389 Outdoor furniture materials are different from the rest. In this case, for example, safety glass must withstand the temperature variation between day and night, also, the color of the coffee table must remain unalterable as it is ceramic.

0390 A terrace on the second floor of the home adds an additional outdoor space. Its good location right next to the master bedroom converts it into a corner that gives the owners some privacy.

0391 The structures, foundations and support materials must be chosen carefully to ensure the stability of buildings. This tree house and its tatajuba wooden terrace 4 m (13 ft) above ground level have been possible thanks to the high quality metal support structure.

0392 Why not sleep on the terrace if it's hot? No one dictates what you can and what you cannot do in outdoors spaces. This canopy bed or pergola with bed, as preferred, offers the option of spending a cool night under the stars.

0393

0394

Balcony floor plan

0395

0396

393 The arrangement of plants around the perimeter of the terrace frees the useful floor space without sacrificing vegetation. So you can place sunloungers, fountains and pergolas.

0394 The situation of the terraces defines the circulation patterns and gives importance to the spaces. Here, the terrace is located between the main body of the house and the pool and guest annex, converting this spot into the central point of communication between rooms.

0395 To define the terraces, especially those at ground level, you can use different systems: low walls, hedges, rails etc. Here, a handrail and some wood have been fitted forming a lightweight wall that will support climbing plants in spring.

0396 A shower on the terrace is a pleasant alternative to spend the warmer months at home. This type of installation, whether fixed or portable, is simple and very inexpensive.

0397 Intelligent architecture is that capable of finding solutions in complex spaces. This home, situated on a lot with steep slope, has managed to create a small terrace surrounding one of the façades.

0398 Do not underestimate the use of furniture and other items in the outdoor spaces, as they layout the space. Large pieces of furniture, such as sunloungers and parasols, give life to urban roof terraces.

0399 After studying the site, it was decided that the under cover areas were underused due to the excessive sun exposure and lack of connection with the lower levels. A new terrace was created that breaks through these schemes and increases the useful surface area of the house.

0400 If you want plants on the terrace but want do not want to bother with complex installations of flowerbeds and problems of damp beds and irrigation, install large, stylish and functional flowerpots.

0397

0398

0399

Diagram

0400

0401

Floor plan

0402

0403

0404

0401 The connection between this home and the small terrace on the second floor is enhanced by bellowed glass doors that practically make the boundaries non-existent. When the doors are open, the difference in wood marks the boundary between the interior and exterior.

0402 The choice of exterior materials, their characteristics and quality are important for calculating the amount of maintenance that the home will require. Here Siberian larch wood, highly resistant to weather inclemencies, has been used for the façade and terraces.

0403 Despite its small size, the successful distribution of this simple terrace can make use of the exterior and take advantage of the famous Parisian rooftops. The Trust in Design designers have developed a small but original space that has a table and even a recliner.

0404 Do not underestimate the importance of installing safety features in the outdoor spaces in your home. In this case, the unevenness of the land and a few metal bars that surround the perimeter of the house keep animals away.

0405 To ensure good communication between interior levels and spaces, terraces and balconies can be built. Visual communication and movement between rooms will be significantly improved, as in this Japanese residence, with multiple terraces on its different floors.

0406 The minimalist design defines the layout of the outdoor spaces of this prefabricated home, which can be installed in multiple locations. An extension of the house forms a narrow but useful terrace which may be combined with the space available in each case.

0407 Materials are indispensable to define outdoor spaces. The difference between the pool area and the solarium is defined with stone for the water area and wooden planks for the terrace.

0408 In this home by the sea, two functions are combined in one element: foundations and terrace in one wooden platform. Thus, extending the outdoor area and providing more stability to the construction of the house.

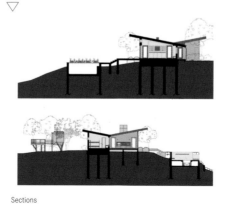

Sections

0409

0410

0411

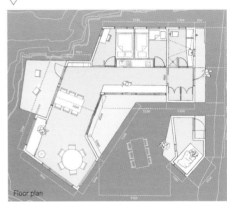

Floor plan

0412

0409 To make the most of outdoor spaces (terraces, pools, gardens, etc.) it is always interesting to place them on the façade facing the landscape so that they are surrounded by nature, making them more spacious.

0410 The orientation of the house has created plenty of outdoor spaces from the strong wind from which to enjoy the rocky landscape and the sea. These spaces offer a more direct contact with nature. The guest annex also helps to deflect prevailing air currents.

0411 If you want to project a terrace using minimum materials demarcate the area with paving that differentiates it from the natural environment. In this case, for example, the wooden platform attains a visual continuity that distinguishes the terrace area from the garden.

0412 Overhangs are one of the best solutions to protect terraces from rain and sun. Unlike awnings and sunshades, they are fixed and more resistant, and a study of the orientation of the house will know what the exact extension of these architectural elements must be.

0413 A few changes can transform a small roof into a cozy chill-out zone. Here, ipe wood covers the setting, the bathtub becomes a mini-pool and the sofa bed is the place to rest from which to enjoy views of the city.

0414 These terraces designed by Franklin Azzi Architecture for this second home in Normandy have the dual function of a porch and terrace. They can also be covered with tarps and increase the useful floor area without violating construction regulations.

0415 The latest trends in residential architecture enhance the use of outdoor spaces throughout the year. To achieve this goal, heating and insulation systems are usually installed on the terraces: movable walls, fireplaces, etc.

0416 It is important to make use of the architectural enforcements of the spaces: the levels of the terrace have allowed the architects to organize the outdoor spaces. The swimming pool and solarium are located at a higher level and along with an access door, a small exterior room.

0417

0418

0419

Axonometric

0420

0417 The layout of the wings of a home can create spaces that improve the connection between the interior and exterior of the house. Here, a comfortable and shaded courtyard has been created thanks to the arrangement of the eaves of the roof, forming an L-shape next to the housing block.

0418 The whitewashed interior walls and light-colored concrete floor in this courtyard is one solution to lessen the impact of sunlight without installing awnings.

0419 The backyard of this house in London has been transformed into an atmospheric outdoor dining area thanks to two simple elements: a glass roof for the dining area and a pond that conveys peace and tranquility.

0420 Install a fireplace to be able to lengthen the seasonal use of the outdoor space. In the courtyard of this home in Montecito a bonfire heats the outdoor living environment.

0421 Although it may seem underutilized, courtyards next to the main entrances have a lot of potential. Here, it has been the perfect solution to create a space to welcome guests and visitors.

0422 With a few details, a little vegetation and stones on the site can transform the small courtyard next to the bathroom into a Zen garden that ventilates the room and gives it personality.

0423 A good solution to lighten the interiors of the homes, especially if they have several levels or if they are between party walls is to have an interior courtyard, which will improve the lighting and ventilation of the rooms.

0424 This stylish courtyard has comfortable beds that form a meeting corner despite the difference in level that separates them. This is an example of how the furniture can help create environments, especially in courtyards designed in an austere manner.

0425

0426

0427

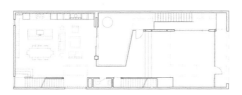

Floor plan

0425 Besides functioning as a light entry between the kitchen and lounge, two high-traffic areas, this courtyard offers a play area for the children of the house: a place to cool off in summer and to shelter from the wind in winter.

0426 To make better use of an interior courtyard, decide what kind of activities you want to carry out in the space. If you want a play area, use resistant materials and leave free space, if you want to install a dining room, better organize the space and choose the right furniture.

0427 The glass enclosure of the interior courtyard of this house in Venice, California, is the perfect solution to introduce natural light into the house and to connect the two public spaces of this floor, kitchen/dining room and lounge.

0428 A good layout of the main bodies of the houses is what can determine the presence or absence of courtyards. A courtyard with an outdoor dining space and a medium-size pool both fit into this space.

0429 Japanese cities are densely populated, so having green space is a luxury available to very few. In this Suppose Design Office project the courtyard has been integrated into the interior design and has created a kind of "room for the plants' surrounding the lower floor.

0430 If you have an interior courtyard and want to prevent water from entering the house, the best option is to use safety glass. This will improve the insulation but will not hinder the entry of light into the other rooms.

0431 To prevent an interior courtyard from becoming a bland space, combine materials and textures. In this house, gravel has been alternated with slabs of pure white stone. The vegetation achieves the desired calming effect.

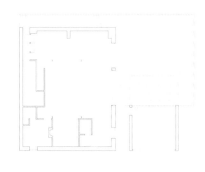

Floor plan

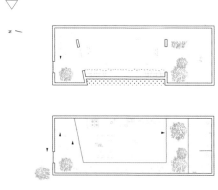

Floor plans

0432 Although the materials are few and simple, their layout can create an interesting and dynamic space. The cedar wood slats on the floor of this courtyard, for example, provide movement to the space and the bright green color adds vitality.

0433 The tradition of courtyards in homes is found in almost all civilizations and cultures: Mediterranean, Japanese, etc. To find the solutions that best suit the tastes of each owner, you may only need to review the local architecture.

0434 To escape conventionalisms play with the interior and exterior concepts and achieve surprising results. This courtyard covered with a large skylight, for example, can be confused with a garden because of the grass.

0435 To enjoy outdoor spaces without having to store furniture every night, choose resistant outdoor furniture, such as those designed by Patricia Urquiola with an aluminum structure, a material that is virtually impossible to corrode.

0436 Pergolas are structural elements that are installed to hold up plants. As they grow they will form a leafy porch that will cool the environment and provide shade in summer.

0437 A pergola is one of the most versatile external elements and they are highly desirable if you want to install one of them in the garden. They can serve several multiple solutions for the exterior; the most common are dining areas, lounges or chill-out spaces either as an extension of the house or next to the pool.

0438 The choice of one material or the other for the support elements of the pergolas and porches, regardless of their technical characteristics, will define the overall aesthetics of space. For example, wood painted dark green and brick create a classic setting.

0439 If you do not want to carry out complex work on the house, install pieces of furniture to decorate the outdoor spaces and increase their uses, such as a mobile pergola to create a chill-out or shaded area on a terrace.

0436

0437

0439

0438

0440 In this new home in Pacific Palisades, California, the outdoor spaces have been carefully designed. The location of the house and the landscape define the layout of the pool, garden and pergola, which eventually will form a vegetation shade without obstructing the view.

0441 It is not necessary to cover an entire space with pergolas and porches. The alternation of sunny areas with shady spaces is the best option if you want to combine various outdoor activities throughout the day.

0442 If the lot is small and is delimited by high fences or walls, make use of spaces created between the perimeter of the garden and the house by installing a pergola, which will create a more intimate ambience.

0443 Attention to detail is what makes the difference in majestic homes. In this case, a pergola completes the semicircular space, which welcomes you into the home, designed by the renowned architect Mark Dziewulski.

0444 The majority of pergolas provide shade thanks to vegetation, especially if climbing plants are used. It is really only necessary to give them a small support, wires, wooden slats etc and give them time.

0445 Small removable lightweight constructions, such as this pergola suitable for outdoor dining is the perfect solution for creating temporary spaces, either for private or for use only in the warmer seasons of the year.

0446 The choice of vegetation for pergolas and gardens does not need to be distinguished from what can be found in the immediate natural environment, in this way the plants are better adapted to the climate and need less care.

0447 Architectural elements such as awnings, pergolas and rails can be adapted to the aesthetics of the home. If you can't find the style you want on the market, ask an architect or carpenter to design one according to your taste.

0448 Outdoor spaces can establish the character of a home with a more or less sculptural appearance. In this case, an eye-catching entrance pavilion to the Kona home is inspired by a traditional local basket weaving craft in Hawaii.

0449 If you have enough space and your budget stretches, a pergola by the pool is a good idea to extend the time spent outdoors without sacrificing comfort. In this Long Island home, a dining room or outdoors living room can be installed, for example.

Floor plan

0446

0447

0448

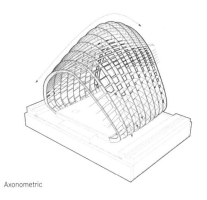

Axonometric

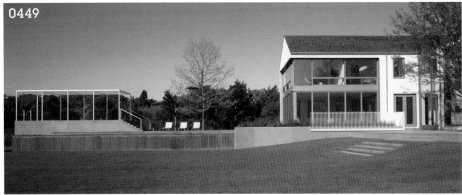

0449

0450 The apparent simplicity of Japanese gardens and courtyards conceals a complex philosophy of relationships between man and nature. The recreation of these areas in a home requires some prior knowledge of this ancient tradition, so it is advisable to seek advice.

0451 A good idea to delineate areas of the garden and protect the grass and plants is to lay slabs on the floor that define the passageways, as in this garden with circular stones.

0452 A zigzag gravel path marks the route through the garden. Textural changes are a good idea when you do not have a large budget for planting vegetation.

0453 The landscape architecture requires a broad knowledge of vegetation suitable for every climate and strategies for recreating environments. In this California home, the spaces are adapted to the vegetation, whatever it may be; the result is a Japanese-style garden.

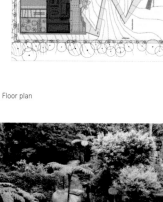

Floor plan

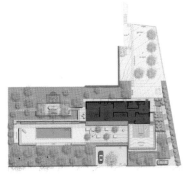

Floor plan

0454 The garden of this Portuguese home has a very simple design. Practically everything is on the same level: the floor of the exterior area of the home, the lawn and pool. This continuity and the limited presence of trees and plants create a serene and peaceful ambience.

0455 The outdoor spaces of the Scoon home merge with the natural environment surrounding the house. Earth tones were chosen for the floor covering and the vegetation is arranged in a seemingly random way, so that does not contrast with the landscape.

0456 The combination of visual elements can be the key to achieve an orderly and balanced garden like this, where shrubs are mixed with freshly cut grass and stone slabs that mark the spaces.

0457 The paths of the gardens, especially when they are lush and thick, can break the sought continuity. To avoid this, create paths with elements that are integrated into the landscape such as irregular slabs, changes in texture of materials, etc.

0458 The rear façades and courtyards of residential buildings are often forgotten about by designers. This has not been the case here: the bamboo garden fills this interior garden with vitality and transforms it into a meeting place for the neighborhood.

0459 The garden of this home crosses the existing space between the main house and studio. To the back, further away from the street and with more privacy, a larger space opens up, combining grass, trees and a wooden floor terrace.

Floor plan

0460

0461

0462

0463

0460 Combining a modern architectural design with a traditional garden is a good option to create harmonic contrasts. The straight-line geometry of Kuro House generates an attractive visual impact with the gentle location of the plants and rocks in the Japanese garden.

0461 To make the most of outdoor spaces, have a small decorative garden at the main entrance of the house and leave as much space as possible in the front part, which may be used by the family.

0462 To create specific paths within the large gardens, build bridges, dining areas, arbors or viewpoints. These elements will configure paths that will lead guests through the most beautiful spaces in the garden.

0463 It is common to use outdoor spaces for household tasks on a daily basis: hanging out clothes is one of the most common tasks. To avoid breaking the aesthetics of the gardens opt for original designs that help to create an attractive image.

0464 The presence of small elements defines the uses that owners want to give their gardens: meeting place, play area, meditation... In this case, a stone bench offers a place to rest and granite stones, placed seemingly at random, are thought-provoking.

0465 A good garden and outdoor space layout will encourage their use and connection with the interior rooms of the house. The garden, courtyards and porches of this luxury Australian home are actually extensions of the interior.

0466 Flower gardens are the best solution to provide more color and vitality. It is true that they require more maintenance and transplants are more frequent, due to different flowering times, but the results are always spectacular.

0467 The garden in this home facing a river covers the entire central courtyard and roof construction. This solution can extend the outdoor surface and create movement between the interior and exterior. Thus, the owners use the gardens a lot more.

0468 The design of a garden defines its function: a place to reflect in, go for a walk, escape to, play in or to carry out your daily chores outdoors. The installation of these daybeds has transformed this part of the garden into a comfortable sundeck.

0469 To avoid the monotony of the walls surrounding the lots, experiment with the organization of the vegetation in the garden. Here, the seemingly irregular arrangement of hedges and trees break the austerity of the concrete and energize the space.

0470 The installation of automatic irrigation, either by a sprinkler system or drip irrigation, is one solution that simplifies and reduces the time spent maintaining the garden.

0467

Sketch

0468

0470

0469

0471 A bonfire area marked by gravel and stones is a decorative accessory for a garden. However, extreme precautions need to be taken to prevent fire from spreading and creating a hazard.

0472 The hours of sunshine and shade must be studied in order to position the outdoor dining areas, especially if you want to use it as much as possible in summer. Here, the outdoor dining area is located in a corner of the rear garden, on a delimited area with gravel under a large tree.

0473 Landscaping in residential developments and neighborhoods faces different challenges than single-family homes. The option chosen in this development has been to design a park that requires little maintenance: several constructed landscape elements and sparse vegetation.

0474

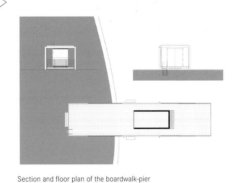

Section and floor plan of the boardwalk-pier

0475

0476

0477

0474 This small outdoors space, a mix between a pier and arbor provides an ideal place to practice water-based activities. To minimize the impact on the land, the platform has minimal contact with the ground and is projected over the water.

0475 A simple and inexpensive way to create a porch is to cover the space between two volumes of a building. You only have to extend the roof.

0476 Any corner under cover can become a stylish porch or rest area with a little resourcefulness. The Japanese aesthetic of the small porch has been achieved thanks to a few details: Japanese calligraphy, a paper lantern and a bamboo bench.

0477 Porches can accommodate multiple functions and can connect interior spaces in different ways, depending on where they are located. In this case, the connection with the guest annex kitchen through a wall of sliding panels stands out.

0478 Do not neglect the wishes of the owners when designing outdoor spaces. They can prioritize issues such as the size of the outdoor area over other issues such as privacy. This porch was designed taking into account the views of the ocean.

0479 The porch canopy has an exposed frame and materials. This feature provides shade in summer and shelter from rain, it increases the available floor space for its occupants. The sliding glass wall connects the interior with the exterior.

0480 The main façade is the one that receives more light, as it faces east. It is precisely beside this façade where a porch was built. From here the garden area, where the children play can be easily monitored.

0481 A family home can save on comfort and livability if outdoor spaces are designed rationally. The central courtyard and porch that divide the house into two can open more windows and create cross ventilation.

0482

0483

0484

0485

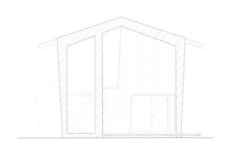

Cross section

0482 The special features of this houseboat, with the main rooms on the top floor, have led to the creation of spaces around the ground floor next to the water. This solution has merged two spaces: pier and porch.

0483 To enhance the flow of air and views of the landscape an opening was made in one of the walls that limit the outdoor dining area located in the pool house.

0484 The location of the porch on the south façade responds to the design, which takes the orientation of the house and use of natural light into account. Porches offer some protection from weather and allow for a more continuous use of outdoor spaces.

0485 The type of space that is formed with the construction of a porch supports multiple possibilities. This porch, which contains a kitchen-barbecue, has a glass roof, and serves as a transitional space between the interior and exterior of the home.

0486 An outdoor dining area is a good solution that is usually installed on porches. In this case, it has a barbecue, a lounge area and a built-in fireplace. In addition, sliding glass panels join this space to living-dining room inside the house.

0487 In families with small children, an outdoor play area can be designed. An area with sand, gravel or grass next to the home's porch. This makes it easier for parents to supervise them without having to stop their activities.

0488 To create additional outdoor space, the architects of this Mexican house have chosen to add a new level in the concrete construction and situate a simple porch on the roof.

Floor plan

0489

0490

Floor plan

0491

0489 Textile items are the perfect choice for creating covered outdoor spaces. These synthetic fabrics move by a few rails placed on steel beams and expand the living area on rainy or sunny days.

0490 To gain space in this urban townhouse in Argentina, the functions on the first floor were limited and priority was given to the garden, pool and this porch that are located between the garage and kitchen.

0491 Eastern architecture is a good example for planning porches and covered outdoor spaces, especially if the climate of the area is hot and wet as in Southeast Asia.

0492 Greens mixed with yellows create a different harmony to pink or orange based colors, although they are fresher and brighter, they equally form warm spaces.

0493 The use of highly saturated warm colors on the walls should be combined with other more neutral and softer colors in the other elements of the room. This prevents the room from appearing visually smaller.

0494 Changing the color palette can transform a minimalist interior into a warm and comfortable living room. If white creates a certain sense of coldness, colors from the range of pinks and burgundies add intensity and elegance.

0495 Orange colors, among which peach stands out, are suitable to create cozy spaces. To avoid an overpowering caramel-toned aesthetic, it is important to dose the quantity and saturation of these colors.

0496 In the transformation of this apartment in Barcelona the living room has been designed as the centerpiece, a key nucleus for the owners. Warm colors with orange as the protagonist were used to emphasize the comfort and the idea of a meeting and reception space.

0497 For a cozy kitchen acid and bright colors may be used, although it is advisable to combine them with other darker colors that strike a balance.

0495

0496

0497

0498 The warmth of wood combined with the color red gives the kitchen a dynamic feel, typical of a family space. The contrast is provided by a pistachio-colored chair that further brightens up the interior.

0499 The almost total lack of furniture leaves the colors responsible for defining the environment. The orange color of the chair and the warmth of the wood create an interior that, despite its bareness, is welcoming and serene.

0500 Red, fuchsia and orange colored wood dominate the interior of this house located in Hawaii. The colors from the red and yellow gamut do not saturate the ambience of the home with the bright Pacific light.

0501 This diagram shows how colors vary the perception of a room and how it can go from being a minimalist studio to a cozy home with the use of warm colors.

0502

0504

0503

0505

0502 The color white is the key to achieving a sober and minimalist atmosphere. To enhance the aesthetic, in this apartment in Amsterdam, white has been used as the main color and superfluous details have been avoided.

0503 The different shades of the wood present in the kitchen, a dark wood for the floor and another lighter brown, together with white, form a very austere space where the colors define the aesthetics of the room.

0504 Grays, especially metallic, create serious and severe spaces; thereby they are a good choice if you seek a sleek, minimalist aesthetic.

0505 To achieve the zen bathroom space sought by the owners, the architects opted for a range of cool colors: blue and gray, which convey relaxation, austerity and tranquility.

0506 Color has an effect on the emotions of people and can contribute to their wellbeing. The choice of neutral colors, such as the gray of the concrete combined with white, transmits serenity and a peaceful ambience in a bathroom, a place designed for relaxation.

0507 The line between elegance and simplicity is very fine and an interior can be completely transformed by only changing a few items or subtly varying the range of colors. Here, the gray interior seating has created a more serious interior design.

0508 An austere ambience can be achieved by the absence of furniture or through the use of a reduced color palette. The simplicity of this living room has been achieved by combining these two concepts.

0509 With the use of only two colors you can achieve a very simple and purely decorative space that radiates personality and enjoy a unique atmosphere, as in the almost monastic aesthetic of this interior.

0510 The range of blues can be used to bring moderation to an interior. Cooler blues convey the serenity and calm necessary in sober spaces. Purple offers an air of sophistication.

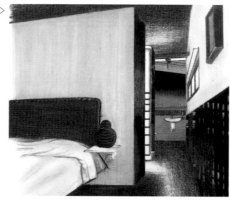

0511

0512

0513

0511 The sobriety of a space is defined by the layout and type of furniture and the colors used. The choice of grays in this apartment creates a harsh and masculine atmosphere, only tempered by the warmth that a bookcase exudes.

0512 Neutral colors from the beige palette have an advantage over other cold and sober colors like gray, and they emanate warmth. These colors convey a sense of comfort even when the rooms are minimalist.

0513 Neutral colors, that provide tranquility, are the protagonists of this apartment in which no color stands out over another in order to exude a sense of balance.

0514 The mixture of whites with other natural shades can create an excessively sober and minimalist space, but when combined with the wooden floor and the classic landscape painting in the bedroom it takes on a distinguished dimension.

0515 The sobriety of the dining room table, couch and carpet, all in neutral tones, is broken with the predominance of the blue-gray to provide a point of warmth to a cold and formal space without detracting elegance.

0516 The materials used for interiors (in carpets, upholstery, etc.) have different light absorptions, which produces interesting variations in the shades of color, in this case, natural, pale tones.

0517 The neo-classical elements of the reception and living room, such as the sofas, lamps and decorative objects, create elegant interiors, but if you want to avoid excessive rigidity use pink colors on the walls and ceilings, thus combining distinction and warmth.

0518 The use of yellow in the headboard and the gold in the mirror frame are the details that contrast with the seriousness of the moldings and the white and add a pleasant warmth to the bedroom.

0519

0520

0521

0522

0523

0519 The predominantly white walls and furniture of this luxury apartment designed by Philippe Starck have been chosen to create a uniform and neutral space with a touch of glamor.

0520 The ideas associated with colors can be used to define the interior of a house. In this case, blue, associated with water, has been used to identify and pinpoint the location of the bathroom.

0521 If you want to avoid excessively austere interiors, use a warm color. The maroon color of the kitchen adds a certain warmth, but without losing elegance.

0522 The combination of three colors is effective as long as the darkest shade does not dominate. In this case, light beige unites the space, the mahogany color works as a secondary color while the hint of orange breaks the duality and adds a touch of freshness.

0523 It is well known that the color green transmits serenity. In this bedroom the combination of olive green with dark brown is reminiscent of Eastern aesthetics and brings an air of elegance to the space.

0524 If you want the bedroom to be a room for relaxation and rest, opt for gray colors that convey serenity and seriousness, although it is advisable to limit the use of these colors and to take care of the decorative details so as not to create impersonal spaces.

0525 Dark colors add solemnity and are suitable to create elegant surroundings. In this case, brown can transform a nondescript and austere room into an inviting and elegant bedroom.

0526 The color violet, which derives from blue and red is an elegant color that adds vitality to this interior in which cold colors stand out. This combination transmits balance and a certain degree of solemnity.

0527 Neutral colors are suitable if you want to make unique decorative items stand out such as furniture design, original lamps, artwork, etc.

0524

0525

0526

0527

0528

0529

0530

0531

0532

0533

0528 The colors from the violet and eggplant range are warm and sophisticated. This makes them ideal for creating glamorous and even sensual interiors.

0529 Burgundy is used to provide warmth to a space which, owing to its dark colors and large size was too formal. The use of a warm color in a cold environment breaks the coldness.

0530 Blue tones create a serene contrast with the dark shades of the wood such as mahogany or cherry. In this apartment elegance is created by the combination of soft shades of blue with the dark floor.

0531 The most effective way to create an elegant yet contemporary space is to combine white with a neutral color palette: beige, sand, etc. In this room, for example, the result is a bright space with clean lines.

0532 A multitude of combinations can be created with white. The color or colors that are combined, in most cases, are what adds character to the room. The dark brown Brazilian walnut adds elegance and balance.

0533 The colors chosen for this apartment transmit peace and create a relaxed atmosphere, like almost all shades of the range of blues.

0534 The originality of the furnishings and the use of blue, a color that stimulates and conveys freshness, have given this dining room a dynamic and lively personality.

0535 Red, used in the beams and the column that forms part of the structure of the apartment, achieves a revitalizing effect and offers a touch of color that modernizes the apartment, which would otherwise be too formal.

0536 The use of bright colors to define spaces requires courage. The orange color of this dining room accentuates the dynamism of the home and transmits the vitality of its tenants. The combination with more sober colors strikes a certain balance.

0537 Three elements have transformed a living room with a classic layout into a space where the atmosphere is more informal: the orange color of the chairs, the leopard-print cushions and an eye-catching picture of Greek amphoras.

0538 To create informal and relaxed spaces the best resource is to use multicolored fabrics, especially in bright colors that combine the warm shades of red and pink with other cooler colors such as greens or violets.

0539

0540

0541

0542

0543

0539 The white background is very effective to make a few selected elements stand out with small hints of color. In this home, the color red defines the informal nature of the space.

0540 As in the living room, hints of color are also used in the bedroom of this home by John Barman. In this case, splashes of yellow and bright red completely break the sobriety of the black.

0541 Wood was used in many of the surfaces of this house to prevent that the double height of this kitchen creates a cold space. The contrast with the apple green provides vibrancy without taking away from the warmth.

0542 Orange colors convert any room into a comfortable and lively space, but they should be combined with other darker tones. This color is suitable for kitchens, small rooms or any family room.

0543 Red is a powerful and intense color that, when used in moderation, as in this apartment where it is combined with white, can result in cheerful interiors that are not overly stimulating.

0544 Acid and bright colors such as yellows and greens help to create a cool and light atmosphere: a good choice for areas that demand clarity and neatness, such as bathrooms.

0545 When using pink and fuchsia in an interior and in such a profuse way, an extremely lively and vital ambience is created.

0546 Bright colors from the range of warm colors transmit energy and give a positive air to the space. In this bathroom, the color pink gives you the burst of energy you need to start the day.

0547 If you want to use saturated colors across a room, such as the red on these walls and ceilings, it is important to have good lighting, both natural and artificial, as the saturation will absorb the light.

0548 To choose the right color palette for a house, sketch each room and try out the various options. It is a laborious task but it can help you make your decision.

0549 Warm colors (yellows, reds, ochres, etc) detract seriousness from interiors and are best suited to create family atmospheres in living rooms, kitchens and casual dining areas.

0544

0545

0546

0547

0548

0549

0550

0551

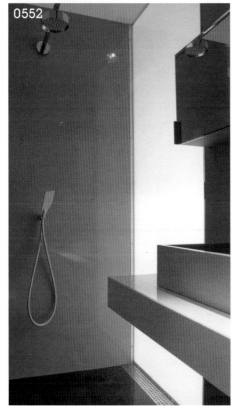

0552

0553

0550 To play it safe, do not use more than three colors in the one room: one or two main colors and a third that adds hints of another shade. In this case, the main color is that of the wood, combined with splashes of soft orange and warm olive green.

0551 To add vitality to a room opt for elements that work as a union between the different colors. The color violet in the chair goes with gray in its cold spectrum and red in its warm spectrum.

0552 The appearance of a bathroom can be changed radically with hints of acid colors on a white or neutral background. They will convey freshness and create a more youthful aesthetic.

0553 The predominant colors are yellow, orange and purple that are alternated in the rooms. The warm palette of colors makes this home with straight lines and austere furnishings less serious.

0554 It is normal to create a cheerful environment that is not overly stimulating in children's bedrooms. In this New York apartment, two primary colors have been used: pink, a positive and sensitive color and lime green, a fresh but balanced color.

0555 The use of blue and pink to differentiate girls and boys bedrooms is a trend that thankfully has fallen by the wayside. To achieve dynamic and cheerful interiors the best option is to mix colors and be daring.

0556 Children's bedrooms stand out for the use of bright colors, albeit with some moderation. In this case we have opted for a colorful padded wall that identifies this space from other rooms.

0557 As children get older, their tastes also change and you should consult them when giving their bedroom a face lift. One option is to use a neutral color and add splashes of color to the decorative objects and bedding, which is easier to replace.

0558 You can use color as a strategy to differentiate spaces. The children's area, located on the third floor of this home, has been painted metallic orange and differs from the rest of the house, painted pure white.

0559 In children's rooms, colors should be used sparingly. In addition to brightening up the room, you should provide a suitable environment for relaxation. Here, we have achieved a serene space with the use of a blue sky.

0554

0555

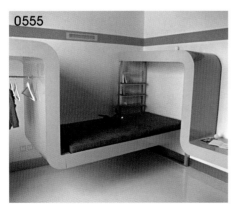

0556

0557

0558

0559

0560 Work spaces should encourage concentration and should be bright. The choice of warm wood and the color white ensures these two premises and creates a cozy study.

0561 White, gray and black is a foolproof way to achieve an elegant work environment, but it is important that the dark colors are not the protagonists. In this case, gray conveys seriousness and white luminosity.

0562 The continuity of the rooms and use of white and red in this apartment are the central themes of this design. Moreover, the use of glass favors the dominance of white in the interior, whether it is in the kitchen, dining room or study.

0563 Excessive colors may be counterproductive in a work space, especially if you spend a lot of time in it. The uniformity of light and warm colors favors a more orderly and calm ambience.

0564 Although the design of this study is unusual, the use of the color green on the walls and furniture should be noted. Green brings serenity and aids concentration, thus it was considered appropriate for this room.

0565 The choice of earth colors and the combination of light and dark tones make the straight and uniform lines of the furniture stand out. The combination of all these elements results in a rational workspace.

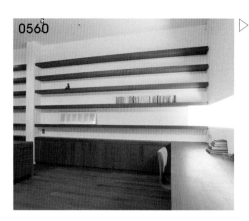

0560

0561

0562

0563

0564

0565

0566 If the pattern repeats the color scheme of a room, black and white in this case, it will achieve this duality and act as a link between the two tones.

0567 Patterns give character to the rooms without the need for striking furniture. This small studio would be a sober and bland space if not for this wallpaper, which gives it a cheerful air.

0568 Patterns and colors are used to create a retro aesthetic environment. In this case, the red carpet, fabric curtains, cushions and chairs transport us to the 60s.

0569 Patterns are a useful way to provide a specific personality to the rooms of a house. They are already in use in the walls or textile items such as curtains, cushions and upholstery, colors and patterns must be chosen that avoid the saturation of the space.

0570

0571

0572

0573

0570 Patterns are a resource to be used with caution as they may produce unwanted effects such as visual saturation. In this case, the application of the same pattern in different colors creates a dramatic effect.

0571 The search for new combinations that surprise and break the monotony and repetition is a constant feature in the work of Karim Rashid. Here the idea of creating strong contrasts of shapes and colors is developed.

0572 Patterns, even if they are not especially striking, add a hint of enjoyment to rooms, such as the kitchen and bathroom cabinets, which are more dynamic through the optical illusion drawings.

0573 Getting the location of a pattern within the room right is the key to creating a specific environment. In this case, a large-format print above the headboard creates an original and modern interior despite its classical theme.

0574 The combination of white and black always creates elegant, urban and modern interiors. Here, the contemporary ambience has been reinforced by the choice of furniture and its arrangement.

0575 The analogous color scheme, i.e. close to each other on the color wheel creates a harmonious atmosphere. In this bathroom, a sand color dominates the space and yellow brings the vital and dynamic touch.

0576 Harmonic colors are found beside each other on the color wheel. In this dining room shades of blue and green are used, although they are not strictly harmonic, they have a certain accord and form a cheerful atmosphere.

0577 A powerful wall is the centerpiece of this apartment in Shanghai. The harmonic range of reds and violets adds intensity, depth and great strength to this individual space.

0578 The orange and red colors are harmonious, which are contiguous in the chromatic scale. Here, orange dominates the setting as it is present in the walls and one of the cushions. Red increases the vitality of the space and light color of the wood unites the ensemble.

0579 Natural colors are part of a big family: ocher, sienna, sand, earth ... The combination of these colors always produces a relaxed space, which is the effect sought by the architects for this home spa.

0580

0581

0582

0583

0584

0585

0580 Green and fuchsia are complementary colors that completely transform a space. Thanks to these bright colors the space can go from bland to cheerful, vital and youthful.

0581 Complementary colors can play a role in revamping an interior. If two complementary colors, such as violet and green, and red and blue like in this room are used, the result is fresh and young even though the furniture and the distribution are more traditional.

0582 Blue and orange are complementary colors and their use in this minimalist design space adds strength and personality. The unity is provided by the sand color of the floor and the sofa which is combined with the two other colors.

0583 If you want to give a room a dynamic style use color schemes such as complementary colors. The strong green color becomes the focus point and creates a strong contrast to the bedspread and dark colors on the walls.

0584 The color red creates a striking contrast in the interior. The tricolor combination of white, black and gray is altered by the presence of this bright tone that breaks the coldness of the main combination and adds a more youthful note.

0585 The curtains of the apartment in Rome play with the contrast of complementary colors, which always achieves a great visual effect. Orange, blue's complementary color, gains prominence, and the fuchsia in the sofa acts as liaison between the two palettes.

0586 Natural lighting is essential to generate amplitude in small spaces. These two Velux windows on the roof of the attic bedroom fill the room with vitality.

0587 In addition to traditional windows and balconies, achieve more light with openings in the top part of the walls and interior windows. In this home in Melbourne, in addition to the openings in the wall there is another window which allows natural light to flood through to the staircase at the back.

0588 The skylights on the roof increase the natural lighting that the interiors receive. This one, located over the bed, is combined with other indirect light sources such as the one installed with the beams, to form part of the final design of the lighting in this room.

0589 Making use of natural light is essential in countries like Sweden, Norway and Finland. Full advantage has been taken of this attic apartment in Stockholm to install some large windows that illuminate the interior.

0586

0587

0588

0589

0590

0591

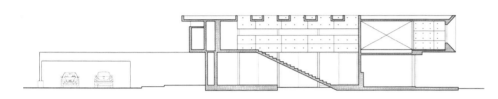

Longitudinal section

0592

0593

0590 The combination of different openings, such as the side windows and skylights of this home create a permanent and dynamic lighting that change throughout the day.

0591 With the right combination of natural and artificial light the right illumination can be achieved for any time of day. In this case natural light still comes through the skylight at sunset with a dim light installed under the elevated space.

0592 Furniture design has a significant impact on the lighting of the rooms, either for its color, which can reflect or absorb light, or due to its form. Here, half-height furniture will allow natural light to cross the study and reach the bedroom.

0593 Sunlight is the best light source there is, so it is vital to take full advantage. At sunset, this room retains its clarity through the light coming from the double open space next to the fireplace.

0594 The annual insolation is lower in northern Europe. To increase natural lighting the architects from Atelier Heiss opted for glass façades and skylights and glass in the stairwell. This solution allows the light to pass vertically through the three-storey home.

0595 Take into account the configuration of the interior, shapes and materials, which affect the lighting. Here, the light that penetrates through this skylight creates long shadows colliding with the cubic and angular shapes of the beams, wall slats and staircase.

0596 Staircases and connecting spaces are ignored in many interior designs. The area around the staircase is finished off with glass, so both natural and artificial light illuminate this small space.

0594

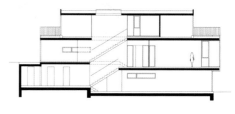

Longitudinal section

0595

0596

0597

0598

0599

0600

0597 The use of glass openings in the extension in the roof has created the sunlight and temperature conditions suitable for creating a garden.

0598 The openings in the top part of the walls, either in the form of operable windows or skylights, increase the brightness of the houses without relinquishing privacy in the interior.

0599 A solution for more efficient lighting inside the home is, for example, is to make some openings in the hallway on the first floor. In this case, the light that enters through windows and skylights reaches the floor below.

0600 For the bathroom area of the master bedroom a glass roof has been installed, as if it were a large skylight. This opening allows you to enjoy natural light all day and watch the sky while relaxing in the bath.

0601 The installation of additional openings in the roof is a good way to bring extra light into the houses. In this case, two models have been installed at different heights.

0602 Skylights located just above the kitchen area provide the lighting for this work area. These strategies that make the best use of daylight have a twofold advantage: to enjoy the benefits of natural light and save energy.

0603 It is always better to take advantage of natural light; it creates more vital spaces that seem larger. The design of this home, which are virtually all the façades are glass, clearly show that they have followed these premises.

0604 Skylights in this home in Belém, Portugal, allow natural light to enter. It is always interesting to study the location of openings and surrounding homes so that owners do not lose privacy.

0605 The openings that have been made taking advantage of the apartment improve the lighting of the rooms without losing privacy. The light passes through spaces and reaches many more corners and the use of transparent and translucent glass ensures privacy in the bedrooms.

0606 The installation of different shapes and sizes of downlights is combined here with a large circular skylight that looks like another larger downlight.

0607 Do not miss the opportunities to renovate spaces. On this occasion, this former industrial warehouse has three original skylights that achieve optimal natural lighting in the living-dining room.

0604

0605

0606

0607

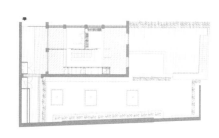

Floor plan

0608 Glass is not the only material that allows light to reach the interior. The use of polycarbonates or other semi-transparent synthetic panels are a good option for permanent openings such as skylights.

0609 The absence of partitions allows for the better illumination of interior spaces, especially when they are small. Thus, the natural light coming through the kitchen window reaches the study area and avoids the use of artificial light during the day.

0610 The use of glass on the floor of the first floor terrace allows light to enter the covered balcony from the lower floor, the composition of the spaces and materials ensure good lighting.

0608

0609

0610

Floor plan

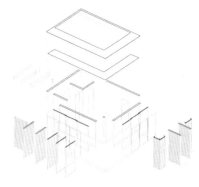

Exploded view

0611 The installation of finger joint pine tilted blinds 50 cm (19 ins) from the glass in the northeast facing walls achieves light and temperature control.

0612 Many elements of a home have dual roles. In this case, for example, wooden shelves next to the glass wall also serve as filters which, according to the time of day, leave the main living room in semidarkness.

0613 Daytime areas do not need as much darkness as bedrooms, so Venetian blinds in the living room windows is a good option to filter the light.

0614 The design of the blinds can be adapted to the needs of each room. The slats of this model, designed by Project Orange, have several positions that can graduate interior light.

0615

0616

0617

0618

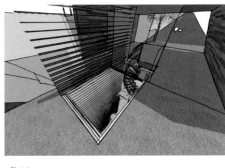

Sketch

0619

0620

0621

0622

0615 Blinds diffuse the natural light and disperse it in a uniform way, thus avoiding the direct impact and sometimes annoying sunlight. In addition, it creates relaxed environments appropriate for work or rest.

0616 Curtains are a perfect solution for changing the light in spaces. Glass walls let natural light into this apartment by Jonathan Clark Architects, but the thick curtains can darken the interior at any time.

0617 The combination of white blinds with bare white walls is the best option to achieve the maximum possible clarity in the studio area.

0618 Strips of Western Red cedar vertically clad the house from the roof to the first floor. These mobile strips regulate the entry and the intensity of light.

0619 The glass block walls, although they are not commonly used, are the best solution to illuminate an interior naturally without losing the thermal properties and acoustic insulation that a conventional wall provides.

0620 The living room of this Mediterranean apartment is a perfect example to explain the diffusion of light through the use of curtains or blinds. With a good choice, the clarity of the room, far from disappearing, multiplies.

0621 Natural light is a great advantage in a home, though it must be filtered to suit the needs of each moment and depending on time of the day. Curtains in fine fabrics control this light and also provide privacy to residents.

0622 The sturdy wooden exterior panels have a dual role in this living room: to filter the incoming light and protect the glass façade.

0623 The façade of this sustainable architecture apartment block incorporates a sun filter with vertical screens covering the balconies and allowing the more extensive use of this space.

0624 The best type of lighting is, without a doubt, natural light. It is an endless resource and its quality is unbeatable. It is also true that its intensity and its direction do not depend on us, so it is necessary to install filters to control it.

0625 There are a multitude of colors and materials, but whites and fine cloths are the best choice to capture maximum natural light even when they are unrolled.

0626 Glass blocks or glass bricks, originally used in industrial areas or civil architecture have been introduced into residential architecture, thanks to they fact they let in light and safeguard the privacy of the interior.

0627 To have the ultimate relaxing bath, play with the lighting of this room. Here, stylish blinds in natural materials leave the bathing area in semi-darkness.

0623

0624

0625

0626

0627

0628

0629

0630

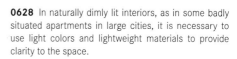

0631

0628 In naturally dimly lit interiors, as in some badly situated apartments in large cities, it is necessary to use light colors and lightweight materials to provide clarity to the space.

0629 Venetian blinds allow you to graduate the amount of light entering the rooms. In places with cold winters, like Slovenia, where this home is located, it is important to capture as much light as possible, but you also need to regulate its intensity.

0630 Blinds and curtains do not have to be secondary elements in the design of a home. Their role is important and may be given more prominence, as in the front of the Japanese house, where bamboo blinds are part of the façade.

0631 The frosted glass installed on the top part of the glass wall filters the light in the apartment and avoids glare without renouncing brightness.

0632

0633

0634

0632 An original solution for the artificial lighting of the house is the resin panels, which can be adapted to the available space. In this Malibu home, for example, this system is used in the space between the living room and kitchen and extends to the terrace.

0633 The use of different colored lights energizes the interior of the room and avoids the monotony of a mostly white room. This lack of color allows the colored light to appropriate the space.

0634 Small lamps have been used to highlight the paintings on the wall in this reception room. The spotlights facing the opposite wall disperse the light, while the opening next to the door, closed with a translucent glass, generally illuminates the space.

0635 Artificial lighting offers multiple combinations that will create different ambiences depending on the taste of the owners. This possibility creates rooms like this apartment with a youthful and lively style.

0636 This fabulous glass façade is another example of how artificial light can escape from the house to spread and illuminate simultaneously the interior and the gardens at night.

0637 The glass walls in the annex allow natural light to enter during the day. At night, when the interior rooms are lit up, the use of exterior lights is reduced and ambient lighting creates a soft and comfortable atmosphere for outdoor dining.

0638 In this room we have designed a soft, comfortable lighting. Indirect lighting under the bed and over the structure of the headboard is combined with two lamps on the nightstands. The curtains that filter light from the balcony complete an intimate atmosphere.

0639 The use of certain colors influences the lighting. If dark colors are used indoors, especially in the kitchen, compensate with powerful, direct lights.

0640 Do not take the difference between light during the day and night lightly, they must be studied together. The outdoor dining area, situated in a glass box, takes advantage of natural light during the day and at night it becomes integrated with the interior thanks to similar lamps.

0641 A sphere-shaped lamp illuminates the dining area of this apartment. Its location, just above the table, provides direct light that means ambient light is not called for in the rest of the room.

0642 This apartment has used the same type of lamps in the study and bedroom. It is a smart choice because both lamps are suitable for working and reading both in a workplace and rest area.

0643 The use of small lamps next to the bed is a widespread resource that allows direct lighting for reading when you are lying on the bed.

0644 One of the difficulties in interior design lies in the relationship between the strategic location of spotlights and the distribution of furniture. In this living room, for example, a balance has been sought between the different halogens lights.

0645 The characteristics of this halogen light model, a powerful and direct light that can be moved to focus on the desired location, are appropriate for this kitchen in dark tones.

0646 To increase the lighting in small spaces like bathrooms, use reflective elements. Installing a recessed fluorescent mirror doubles the amount of light where it is most needed.

0647 Exterior lighting is subject to different specifications from interior lighting. Its components must be approved for outdoor use and sockets and switches must have higher insulation.

0642

0643

0644

0645

0646

0647

0648

0649

0650

0651

0652

0653

0654

0655

0648 The choice of lamps can be the main feature in the aesthetics of the rooms. In the guest bathroom direct lighting was not considered necessary, so we opted for a lamp that generates a very personal theatrical atmosphere.

0649 The integration of ambient lighting in furniture is useful especially outdoors. Installing these lights can save space on balconies and terraces.

0650 Colored lights can play an important role in defining an interior, so think about the implications of their installation. Depending on the color and type of light, direct, diffuse, etc, the space can transform and influence the mood.

0651 Combinations of different types of lamps create ambiences different from the usual. In this case, recessed light fixtures in the ceiling and low lights under the workbench generate an atypical but also functional light.

0652 The use of certain lamps outdoors defines the ambience you want to create. Dimmer lights, for example, highlight a specific area without the need for a powerful, direct spotlight that could be annoying.

0653 The combination of several lamps in the same room creates patterns and changes the perception of the space. Turn on all lights at an informal dinner or just use floor lamps for more intimate occasions.

0654 The owner of this apartment wanted a space with clean, warm lines. To achieve this, the architect Mariano Martín designed a false ceiling that conceals indirect lights, which provide this characteristic diffused light.

0655 The light intensity can be adjusted to achieve the effect sought after by architects and owners. In this case, the frosted glass distributes the blue light from the lamps in a uniform way.

0656 Fire was the first lighting for man who turned a natural element into something artificial. Sometimes it is interesting to remember this; a fireplace can create the perfect lighting at certain times.

0657 The choice of interior materials can influence the ambience of the interior and must be taken into account. The use of wood in walls and the ceiling of this home, for example, absorbs part of the light from the lamps by reducing its intensity.

0658 When designing the interior of a home take into account the distribution of furniture to install the sockets and switches: in this bedroom, you control all the lights from the bed.

0659 To ensure adequate lighting, think in advance about the needs and routines at home. If, for example, you like to watch movies, you may want to install indirect ambient lighting so that the room is darker.

0660 The lighting located under the bed in the master bedroom of this apartment designed by Anthony Chan helps to create a modern, sophisticated and inviting atmosphere.

0661 This apartment in New York, designed by Gary Shoemaker Architects, combines perfectly natural light with different types of lamps. The ambient light surrounding the fireplace and the small ceiling lights can be appreciated in this image, adding brightness to the interior.

0662 Lighting creates stunning effects that can be used to benefit the construction and aesthetics. This elegant and ethereal façade has been achieved thanks to the effect that this powerful white light creates behind the blinds.

0663 The line that separates decoration from the lighting is very fine and this provides another tool to create an interior. The square and colored objects in this dining room include lit up paintings and wall sconces.

0664 Lamps can separate spaces and uses. In this apartment, for example, embedded halogen lights and drawers in the false ceiling define the surface of the kitchen and dining room without the need for partitions.

0665 It is interesting to use resources that fulfil a dual role, such as these lamps, which are also flowerpots. Spaces can win on originality and be much more practical with this type of solution.

0663

0664

0665

0666

0667

0668

0669

0666 Outdoor lighting can be basically functional; the exterior of this home includes small spotlights that mark the entry to the front door and the garage.

0667 This living room has two examples of good ambient lighting: a floor lamp in the middle of the coffee table and lights hidden behind the false ceiling, which together, provide plenty of light without creating a glare.

0668 Illumination is the ultimate resource to highlight elements in an interior. In this case, a false skylight and indirect lights turn a living room into a spectacular theatrical environment.

0669 Floor lamps are used to create additional lighting. This type of warm, spot light usually has two objectives: to reinforce natural lighting and create different ambiences within the home.

0670 Working areas can be the most difficult to light up. Using lamps on the interior and under kitchen cabinets facilitates the location of appliances and the visibility of countertops.

0671 The illumination of an area can be designed with multiple elements and electrical lamps are not always necessary. These objects are an example of how lighting can be complemented without the need for electrical installations.

0672 To create interiors with personality integrate several issues: distribution of spaces, furniture, color, lighting, etc. In these rooms accent lighting fuses with decoration.

0670

0671

0672

0673

0674

0675

0676

0673 Exterior wall lamps are specifically designed with strength and durability. They are used as security elements, to emphasize paths or steps.

0674 Fluorescent lights were the first energy-saving lights that made energy cheaper compared to incandescent lights, and for this reason they were used in industries and offices. Their use spread to residential areas, especially kitchens and bathrooms.

0675 Lamps that can adjust the light automatically or by passing a hand or object over them are commercially available. These systems contribute to visual patterns that create environments.

0676 Halogen lights stand out for their high performance and low power consumption. They produce a large amount of white light, which must be adapted to different spaces to convey the desired ambience without impairing the view.

0677

0678

0679

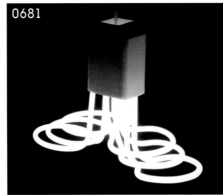

0681

0680

0682

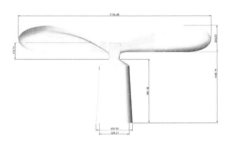

Construction detail

0683

0684

0677 If there are no power sockets outdoors, use solar energy lamps, like this one in the shape of a pot which also uses very low power consumption LED lights.

0678 Downlights are suitable for places that need bright light, as the interior reflects plenty of light and its power consumption is low.

0679 The infinity of lamps on the market makes it possible to define the character of a house depending on the material chosen: clear glass, plastics, textiles, metal, etc., etc.

0680 Incandescent lamps emit a more yellow light. The use of these lamps should be taken into account if you want to create a warm and comfortable interior.

0681 Traditional light bulbs have regular unattractive shapes so they should be hidden behind screens or panels. This design, however, will bring personality to the interior.

0682 Wind power can also be transformed into electricity and light up a space. This original model of lamp includes the blades in the design of the lamp.

0683 These bulbs designed by Felix Stark are the current, fun choice to combine energy efficiency and durability with contemporary interior design.

0684 Fluorescent tubes can be hidden behind semi-transparent screens, thus avoiding direct white light that generates cold ambiences.

0685 The original elements involved in the reforms, such as this vaulted ceiling, are much more notable when combined with contemporary materials and designs. In this way the quality of life is enhanced without losing the nobility of the original architecture.

0686 In renovating this alpine hut a roof was designed with eaves that create a small porch making it easier to move around the outside during the cold and snow while respecting the size and shape of the traditional local architecture.

0687 The restoration project demanded keeping some old ceramic silos embedded in the stone. With the refurbishment, these elements were integrated inside the building and surrounded by a staircase. Windows were also added at the level of the lounge, enabling other remains found in the house to be seen.

0688 The processes involved in renovating a historic space may include treating the wood, replacing the beams, sanitation and repair of the original stonework and insulating the roof.

0689 The alterations combine styles and periods with furniture of contemporary design and traditional materials like wood. In this case, the double opening doors have also been maintained to generate the eternally elegant contrast between the old and new.

0685

0686

0687

0688

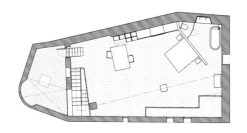

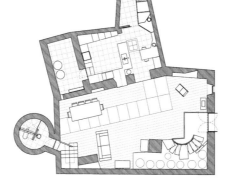

Floor plans

0689

0690 The change of site of the bedroom was brought about by means of a new wall separating the bedroom from the rest of the house. This solution made it possible to link up the day area with that of the water installations without disrupting communication with the other parts of the apartment.

0691 The refurbishment of this 18th-century building located in the historic district of Mantua has led to the recovery of the building's original character, (which was somewhat distorted after several alterations) and to re-establish a new link between the interior of the apartments and the landscaped courtyard.

0692 The reforms help rationalize the layout of the different areas. By distributing the space more efficiently, another bedroom has been obtained for guests, along with a TV lounge. This new layout also enables the kitchen and dining area to be used to divide the space between day and night zones.

0693 This apartment was an open, empty space, without any type of finish. The new layout has achieved a subtle division between public and private zones, while allowing each space to merge with the one adjacent to it.

0694 The facade on this reform project, with outer louvers of aluminum and glass, protects privacy and also an interior that changes according to the time of day and wishes of the owners.

0695 This apartment, in a historic district, has managed to recover the original essence while incorporating a contemporary project tailored to the needs of the owners, without forgetting the requirements of strict heritage protection legislation.

0690

Floor plan

0691

0692

Original floor plan / New floor plan

0693

 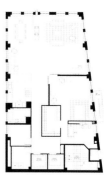

Original floor plan / New floor plan

0694

0695

0696 When dealing with extensions or annexes, architects have more freedom to experiment and play with materials. In this new building, concerning an extension for a house near Hico, Texas, corrugated metal, PVC and cement fiber have been used.

0697 A good time to put up an extension is when carrying out reforms. If all the changes and renovations take place at the same time, savings are made in costs, time and trouble. This extension was carried out when addressing problems on the facade and site of the property.

0698 The owners of this house, which was built in the nineteen forties, were faced with a dilemma: they needed more space but at the same time they did not want to leave the neighborhood. So they decided to extend the property, which had already been initially extended back in the nineteen nineties.

0699 When extending a property, priority should be given to objectives that make it more appealing to live in. In this house in Los Angeles, for example, a space on the ground floor that was in a dark, closed area was converted into a two-story house that faced outwards to benefit from the light.

0700 Extensions may be carried out to improve the amenities, particularly when the intervention includes water installations and the age of the property makes renovation difficult, as is the case in this annex housing the bathrooms.

0701 The extensions enhance the quality of life inside the property. The architects took advantage of the fact that the property needed full restoration to build an annex with a contemporary look that would increase natural daylight and provide direct communication with the back yard.

0702 This impressive studio and exhibition hall is the result of an extension of the main residence. The main element is the floor, which has been cantilevered out to extend the surface area and give the place a more dramatic appearance.

0696

0697

0698

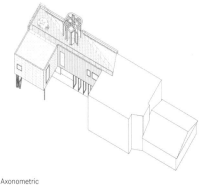

Axonometric

0699

Extension phases

0700

0701

Floor plan

0702

0703 Glass is a main feature in the extension. This enables the interior of the communal areas, which are used more often during the daytime, to receive natural daylight, thereby reducing electricity consumption. The difference between the new building and the old house gives the property a more modern appearance.

0704 An extension to a property can be used to incorporate recycled materials or energy-saving measures, such as those found in this house in Australia, in which the openings in the newly created spaces generate cross ventilation and render air conditioning unnecessary.

0705 Extending a property may provide an opportunity to change its layout and reorganize the spaces in a more advantageous way. In this case, the kitchen and dining room are located between the old house and the new area.

0703

0704

Section

0705

Floor plan

0706

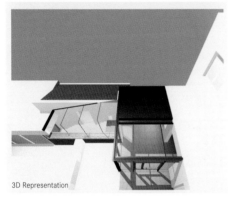
3D Representation

0707

0708

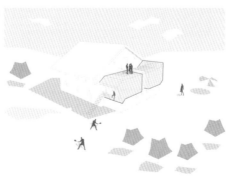
Axonometric

0706 The erection of annexes can solve existing problems in the original building. This new space takes advantage of the difference in level (1.8 m, or about 6 ft) existing between the house and garden to create a transit area housing the new library.

0707 The main house and guest wing can be connected by creating common spaces, such as swimming pools, porches, or outdoor dining areas. In this way, both areas will keep their privacy while being linked together at the same time.

0708 Although in most cases annexes can be accessed from the main building, it is advisable for them to also have a separate entrance even though the two buildings are adjacent.

0709 Annexes allow the surface area to be extended for various activities. The annex to this property meets the entertainment needs of the client, which include a media room, gym, sauna and outdoor kitchen area.

0710 A good solution for extending the surface area of a house is to transfer some of the rooms to a separate space. If you have a large enough garden, a small studio, an annex for guests or a playroom can be built.

0711 The decision to build an annex to the property was due to the awful lighting conditions in the main building. This new space allowed one end of the house to be opened up, thereby gaining space and, above, natural daylight.

0712 If an annex is planned, solutions can be applied to make these spaces adaptable and suitable to be put to various uses. Sliding partitions will be extremely useful for this purpose.

0713 Annexes can incorporate features that will enhance the living conditions or efficiency of the house. In this case, the new terraces have also been used for the installation of solar panels to reduce energy consumption.

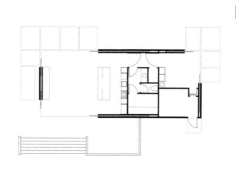

Floor plan

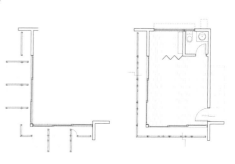

Detail of the panels and floor plan

0711

0712

0713

0714 This refurbishment has transformed a garage into a study and family living room. The beams and columns have been embedded in the new walls but, since the existing structure has been maintained, this necessarily means that there are limitations in the use of materials and the distribution of new applications.

0715 Disused rural buildings, such as barns and stables, need to conform to building regulations if they are to be transformed into homes. In most cases, the requirements relating to safety issues and insulation are greater.

0716 Taking old garages and converting them into studios is a common practice thanks to the adaptability and versatility of such spaces and the fact that they offer a certain amount of privacy since they are not part of the main house.

0717 A good solution for renovating rural estates and avoiding any extension to the existing surface is to transform spaces that have fallen into disuse into rooms forming part of the house. The barn and old farm cottage have been transformed into the living room and guest house respectively.

0718 Transforming industrial warehouses into housing has an advantage: they are very open spaces and allow for a flexible organization of the rooms, which can be adapted to each individual case.

0719 In changes made to the use of the buildings, whether old rural or industrial spaces, there is a tendency to keep the original elements both in and outside, thereby preserving the historical heritage.

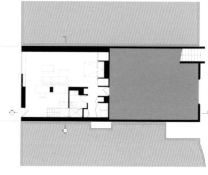

Floor plan

0717

0718

Elevation

0719

0720

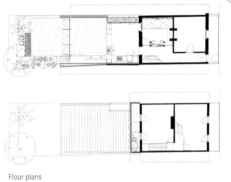

Floor plans

0721

0722

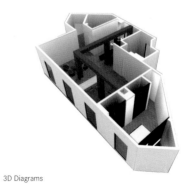

3D Diagrams

0723

0724

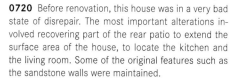

0725

0720 Before renovation, this house was in a very bad state of disrepair. The most important alterations involved recovering part of the rear patio to extend the surface area of the house, to locate the kitchen and the living room. Some of the original features such as the sandstone walls were maintained.

0721 The only original elements that still remain in this apartment are the load-bearing columns. To integrate these in the new design, it was decided to paint them red and create a sharp contrast of color and texture.

0722 The contrast between the rugged stone on the outside of the building and its smooth, stark interiors show how the mix of textures can be a useful tool in renovating rural properties.

0723 The extension of an old farm shows the importance of contrast between the original buildings and those that have been put up more recently. This marked difference is not only important from an aesthetic point of view, but also meets the current needs of the owners.

0724 Despite the fact that the exterior of the building has respected local architectural traditions, the large glass doors leading indoors add a modern touch and show how restoration work can be used to modernize and enhance the original architecture.

0725 The main reason for renovating this apartment in Madrid was to seek out the authenticity of the original architecture, dating back to the nineteenth century. Hence, the priority was to recover some of the original features like the radiators, moldings on the ceiling and woodwork.

0726

0727

0726 If the original construction has a lot of personality or a well-defined style, it is advisable for the new features to blend into the background to ensure they do not impinge upon the traditional architecture. In this case, the glass on the ground floor is fused into the facade.

0727 The transformation of the fireplace has been one of the main features of these reforms. This original element in the house has been kept and is now the main feature in the living room.

0728 The success of combining features from other periods in the reforms lies in balancing the new, which is normally fresh, bright and full of color, with the original, which are still present in the background.

0729 The coexistence of original features with other newer additions when renovations are carried out should not compromise the architectural coherence of the property or its interiors.

0730 Alterations carried out inside the home, involving changes in the use and distribution of the rooms, does not constitute a problem for maintaining the original atmosphere. This property maintains the wooden beams and brick walls thanks to intelligent architectural renovations.

0731 The need to renovate a property can provide an excuse to integrate elements that are not very common, such as the ones in this apartment in Prague. Two cargo containers have been installed on the old roof providing living areas that increase the overall surface area of the property.

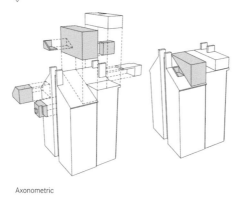

Axonometric

0732 The presence of solar panels requires certain machinery and installations that need to be set up inside the house or on the land, particularly if the panel array is very large. This needs to be taken into account if an installation of this type is decided upon.

0733 The electricity for this project was designed by Resolution: 4 Architecture is obtained thanks to photo-voltaic panels generating 3000 kilowatts. These panels, located quite close to the house, can produce all the energy required by the owners.

0734 The hut is off the grid for practical and environmental reasons. Some photovoltaic panels integrated in the building and other remote panels powered by battery supply enough energy for the lighting and power outlets.

0735 The photovoltaic panels on the roof of this holiday home produce enough power to cover one third of the owners' electricity requirements. Although initially it might seem like a considerable financial outlay, in the long term installing this type of system leads to significant cost and energy savings.

0732

0733

0734

0735

0736

0737

0737

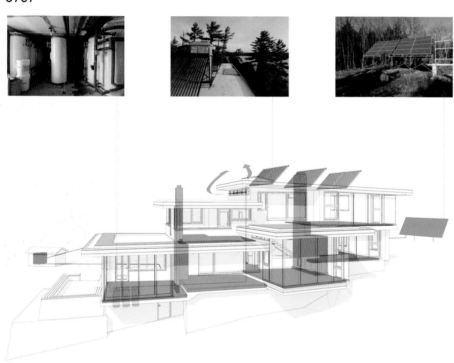

0738

Bioclimatic diagram

0739

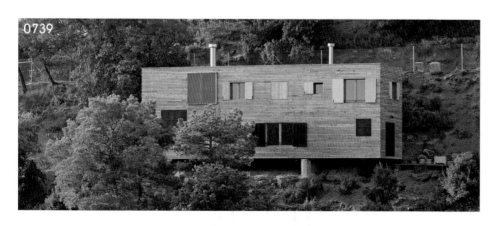

0736 The design of a residential property can combine style with sustainability and energy collection systems can be functional without being visible. The shape of the roof on this house hides the solar panels from the neighbors' view.

0737 The best way to obtain the energy required is by combining various systems. This house, designed by Altius Architecture, has active systems: the photovoltaic panels generate electricity and the thermal solar panels heat water, which is stored in tanks.

0738 The thermal solar panels, which heat the water for use in baths and for heating purposes, should be installed on the side of the roof with greater solar incidence.

0739 An examination should be carried out for the strategic placement of the solar panels, not only to make these systems more efficient, but also to make them blend in with the style of the house. In this case, for instance, the panels look like huge windows.

0740 The combination of active and passive systems can lead to practical win-win solutions: The solar panel array on this house forms a roof that shades the terrace.

0741 This diagram shows how a thermal solar installation works to heat water and power heating systems. From the panel on the roof the water runs into a tank, which is the beginning of the hot water circuit running round the house.

0742 The Truro residence in Cape Cod, Massachusetts, uses three times less electric power than a conventional home thanks to the solar panels installed on the south-facing roof, which enjoys greater exposure to the sun.

0743 Although it may not be possible to rely solely on solar energy, the installation of photovoltaic solar panels does help to reduce consumption of the conventional power supply coming from sources that are not so sustainable.

0740

0741
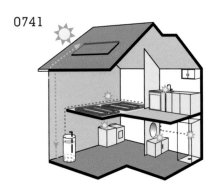

Bioclimatic diagram

0742

0743

0744

0745

0746

0747

Elevation

0744 The proper installation of photovoltaic panels can even send surplus energy to the grid. The solar panels integrated in this roof, covering a surface area of 70 sq. yds), achieve and demonstrate the feasibility of this project.

0745 This prototype for a sustainable home, developed by the University of Illinois, has photovoltaic solar panels installed on the southern side of the roof. These panels produce more electricity than is necessary to power the property's electrical appliances.

0746 Maintenance of the solar panels is easy: if there are no anomalies, all that needs to be done is to rub them down with soap and water, although it may be necessary to call in specialized personnel if they are difficult to get to.

0747 If you want to take the house off the grid and have an independent power supply, these are the two types of most common solar panels that can be installed: photovoltaic panels for electricity and thermal solar panels to heat the water for showers and heating systems.

0748 The function of the tank in this solar panel model on the Chromagen residence is to ensure that the water generated by the collectors stays hot for a limited period of time: between one and four days.

0749 The thermal solar panels with a vacuum tube system, which can be recognized by the cylindrical tubes, are more efficient as they do not contain any antifreeze.

0750 The water which is heated thanks to the solar energy is stored in evacuated tubes with a capacity that should be calculated according to the volume of water used in the house and the capacity of the solar panels.

0751 To obtain a greater yield of solar energy two types of solar panels should be installed: those that generate electricity, i.e. photovoltaic panels, and those that heat water, which are easier to install and also cheaper.

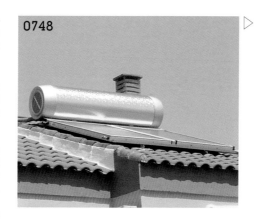

0752

0753

0754

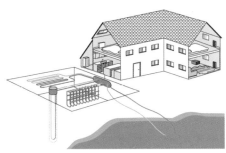

Bioclimatic diagram

0755

0752 Using geothermal energy, which harnesses the heat from the Earth, is less complicated in places enjoying a particular volcanic topography, such as is the case in Iceland. The heating for this residence takes advantage of the heat underground.

0753 Radiant heating is one of the most efficient heating systems, and, even though it is better to have it installed while the house is being built, its subsequent inclusion does not present too many technical problems.

0754 Underground heat is a very cheap source of energy which is worthwile using: it heats the water and this can be used for radiant heating and also in conventional radiators.

0755 If you intend to install a geothermal energy system on a plot of land, you need to have enough space available, as every square foot of housing requires approximately 13 to 21.5 sq ft) of land without any trees growing on it.

0756 The geothermal air conditioning system can also cool the interior of the house thanks to the exchange of temperature: in summer the heat goes below ground and in winter it rises and heats the rooms.

0757 The vertical geothermal installation, which requires drilling down about 330 ft), is more expensive and is normally used to heat housing in urban environments.

0758 To ensure that the temperature is comfortable all over the house a system of wireless thermostats can be installed to control the temperature in each room and regulate the level of radiant heat on an individual basis.

0759 Pipes have been installed underneath the paving on the floor, connected to a geothermal system, which keep it warm in winter and cool in summer.

0760 The choice of heating should be made in keeping with the type of climate in the region and the needs of each family. The combination of thermal mass and radiant heating is the option chosen for this home in California, located in a region enjoying a Mediterranean climate.

0761 The radiant heating system was the first to be connected to the hot water generated by solar panels. To get the most out of this installation, there is a system that also enables cool water to circulate round the house in summer and keep it cool.

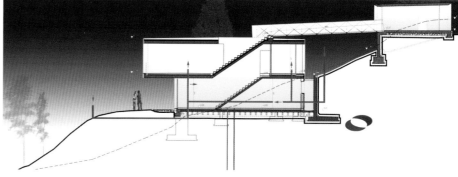

Air mechanical control

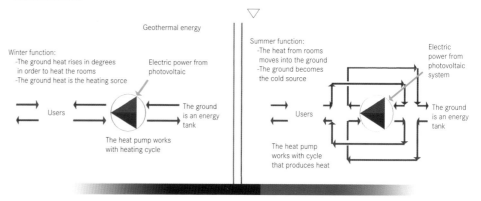

Geothermal energy

Winter function:
 -The ground heat rises in degrees in order to heat the rooms
 -The ground heat is the heating sorce

Electric power from photovoltaic

Users

The ground is an energy tank

The heat pump works with heating cycle

Summer function:
 -The heat from rooms moves into the ground
 -The ground becomes the cold source

Electric power from photovoltaic system

Users

The ground is an energy tank

The heat pump works with cycle that produces heat

Bioclimatic diagram

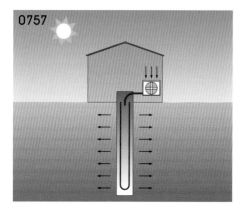

0759

0760

0761

Floor plans

0762 Wind turbines are capable of producing all the electricity required for running a house, even for recharging an electric car, and therefore they might be a good option for supplying energy to remote locations that have problems connecting to the mains.

0763 Regarding maintenance, the various components of the wind turbines should be inspected at least once a year to see if there is any damage.

0764 Studio 804 is a architectural design studio where students from the school of architecture at the University of Kansas are conducting a high-level sustainable design project. A domestic wind turbine is one of the clean energy sources for this home.

0765 To improve the efficiency of the wind turbines, it is advisable to leave a minimum distance of about 10 or 11 yards) to the nearest buildings and trees and avoid sites with excessive turbulence.

0762

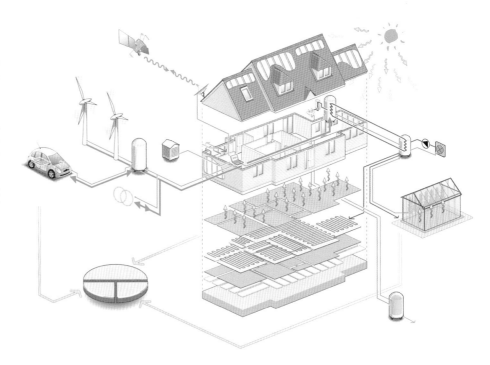

Bioclimatic diagram

0763

0764

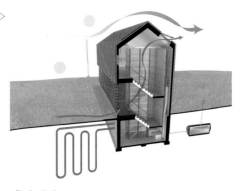

Bioclimatic diagram

0765

0766

0767

0768

0769

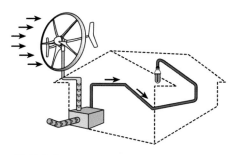

Bioclimatic diagram

0766 If it is intended to install wind turbines on columns, it is advisable to carry out a preliminary study to find out the best location and whether the site is appropriate: if it receives currents of air, if there is enough space around it, etc.

0767 The use of wind turbines is a good option for replacing or complementing solar PV panels, especially in winter or in regions with fewer hours of sunlight.

0768 Apart from consulting the regulations and relevant permits for installing domestic wind turbines, it is useful to know whether local councils offer subsidies for their installation within the context of sustainability and energy savings programs.

0769 The wind turbines work with a seemingly straightforward installation: the most important element after the turbine is the transformer, which converts motion into electricity and adjusts it so that it can be passed on to a conventional electrical installation.

0770 Green heating systems can be combined and alternated for a more efficient HVAC system. Apart from a geothermal heating system, this house also has a biomass heater, which can be lit whenever necessary.

0771 The pellet-burning stove works by sucking in air, which is heated as it passes through the area where the fuel is burning, before exiting again. The smoke is removed by means of a centrifugal extractor fan.

0772 Biomass heaters are based on traditional wood stoves, but with more advanced technology, and are therefore easier to use. Furthermore, combustion is optimized avoiding an excessive use of wood or pellets.

0773 The combination of pellet-burning stoves with thermal solar panels is the best heating option from a financial and environmental point of view.

0774 This lounge is extremely versatile. The fireplace, by Focus, can be turned on itself to face the outside, and the huge sliding window connects the lounge with the terrace. These two features solve the problem of limited space and prolong the season for using the outdoor area.

0775 There are many systems that use biomass energy. However, the most effective ones for a home are those that work with a stove. The energy that is given out by the wood or other non-perishable fuels when burned is used directly for heating the interior of the home.

0776 One of the advantages of having biomass stoves is that CO_2 emissions are deemed to be non-existent. Whether the stove burns wood, as in this Dutch home, or uses pellets, the fuel is considered to be renewable and inexhaustible.

0777 The fireplace, which opens out onto both sides of the lounge, provides heat to both the living and dining areas. A good design and closure of the hearth means that the wood burns better and there is no loss of heat.

0770

0771

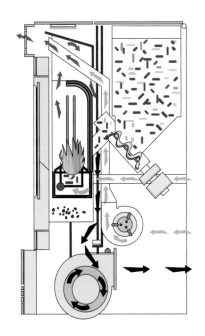

Bioclimatic diagram

0772

0773

0774

0775

0776

0777

0778 These diagrams show the most common methods of generating cross ventilation: the basic principle is to allow the hot air to escape from the residence by being displaced by cool air.

0779 An operable skylight installed in the roof has two functions: to increase the natural light and generate cross ventilation. The air enters through the door and through the windows on the north side and rises to the ceiling. This means that no cooling system is required during the warmest months of the year.

0780 A good idea for regulating the amount of light and heat that enters the rooms is to install blinds with a garage-type opening. These can be raised to a greater or lower height to control the amount of sunlight and let the air in to ventilate the inside.

0778

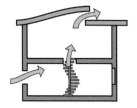
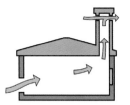
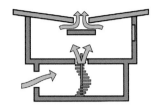

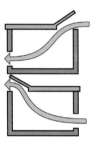
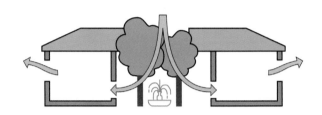

Bioclimatic diagram

0779

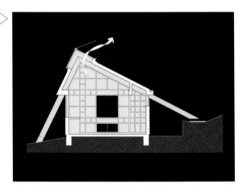

Section: natural ventilation diagram

0780

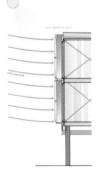

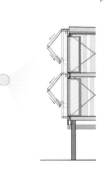
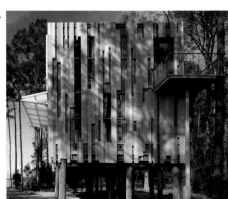

Bioclimatic diagram

0781

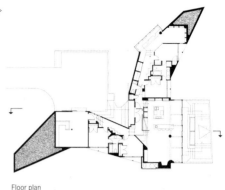

Floor plan

0782

0783

Floor plans

0784

0781 For a good air conditioning system cross ventilation can be used: thanks to a system where air enters and leaves the building, the interior can be cooled or heated without much energy being required.

0782 Las fachadas de esta residencia se han orientado de manera que aprovechan las brisas de la zona; las ventanas laterales permiten la salida del aire y la consiguiente ventilación del interior.

0783 The architectural elements that produce shade and protect the houses from excessive exposure to the sun's rays are the most effective and cheapest solution for stopping the rooms inside from getting too hot.

0784 The dual function of the architectural elements is a good solution for a green lifestyle: the installation of solar panels has generated a covered porch that provides shade during the summer.

0785 Adjustable louvers can be installed on the outer walls receiving the highest solar incidence to prevent the interior from getting too hot without stopping the sunlight from entering in the winter.

0786 A good idea for cooling down the atmosphere and reducing the temperature is to get the air currents to pass over areas of water: ponds, swimming pools, etc. This combination will help cool the air down naturally.

0787 Tropical climates, which alternate between high temperatures and intense rainfall, are ideal for designing spaces whose interior can be cooled down through the use of cross ventilation.

0788 To generate cross ventilation that will cool and renew the air indoors, currents of air can be generated by installing an air vent at the top of the house. The warm air, which is lighter, will escape outside, enabling a cool breeze to enter.

0789 Inner courtyards act like passive air conditioning elements since they alter and control the circulation of air between the inside and outside of the building, and therefore it is interesting to include them in the bioclimatic design strategy.

0790 Courtyards increase the ventilation of single-family homes, especially if the air currents have been analyzed, along with the way of harnessing them, and the air is constantly being renewed in the rooms surrounding them.

0791 Inside, a corridor acts like a heat damper between the glass wall and the bedrooms. An Extira screen, formed by composite wooden panels that are low in formaldehyde, provides shade and stops this transit area getting too hot.

0785

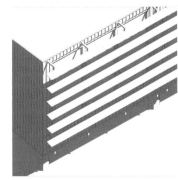

Construction detail

0786

Bioclimatic diagram

0787

0788

0789

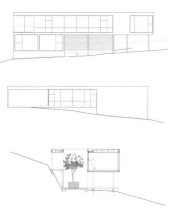

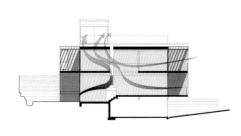

Section: natural ventilation and solar shading diagram

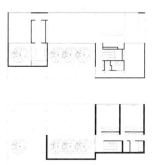

Elevations and section

0790

0791

0792

0793

0794

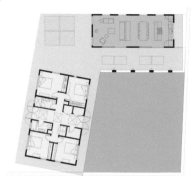

Floor plan

0795

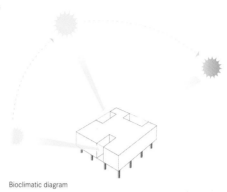

Bioclimatic diagram

0796

Bioclimatic diagram

0797

0792 The presence of trees and awnings is beneficial because it generates shade and filters that protect the house from excessive heat throughout the summer months. The vegetation cools the air around the house and the shade makes it possible for outdoor areas to be enjoyed more often.

0793 The eaves and overhanging elements of the roof provide shade during the summer months. However, this may stop the house from receiving sunlight in winter. To solve this problem, the designers at CCS Architecture have made some openings in this element to stop it losing heat in the coldest months of the year.

0794 A tree in a main courtyard is one of the best systems around for cooling indoor areas in summer, since it provides shade. If the tree is deciduous, like this Chinese elm, it will lose its leaves in winter and allow the sunlight to warm the house.

0795 The shade produced by the sliding panels of synthetic materials cools the atmosphere in two different ways: they cool down the inside of the building when they are closed and create shade and generate currents of air when they are opened.

0796 To ventilate the interior of the house efficiently, one possibility is to place vents strategically around the top part of the house, to allow the hot air to escape.

0797 The fixed slats and eaves, located on the two main facades, enable the amount of heat and sunlight entering the residence to be regulated. The ones located on the southern side are particularly important, since this is the side that receives most heat in the summer.

0798 The harvesting of sunlight to store heat and release it at night may be done in various ways. This residence has been able to collect thermal mass in an original manner: by installing bottles of water on the wall that receives most sunlight during the winter.

0799 The materials surrounding the house - stone and slabs of concrete – generate a thermal mass outside, which can be used on the terrace, allowing such spaces to be used more often.

0800 The concept of thermal mass involving the accumulation of heat to release it hours later, is also known as the greenhouse effect. In this house a large surface of glass allows the sun's rays to enter and heat the rooms inside.

0801 The use of dark colors and solid materials such as stone or concrete is one good option if you want to collect heat using the thermal mass method.

0798

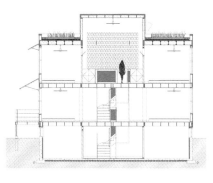

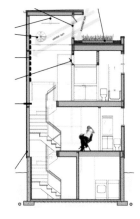

Bioclimatic diagrams

0799

0801

0800

0802

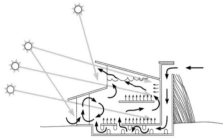
0804

Bioclimatic diagram

0803

0805

0802 Passive air conditioning systems are usually combined with other insulating systems. This property has a concrete platform that stores the heat from the sun, along with a green roof which insulates the inside.

0803 Adapting the houses to the topography of the area has several advantages. One of these is the harnessing of the thermal inertia of the Earth, which helps stabilize the temperatures inside.

0804 In order to collect the sun's rays in winter and be able to use the power generated by the thermal mass, it is imperative to orientate the main facade towards the south and study the inclination of the eaves in relation to the latitude.

0805 Good insulation is the perfect companion for thermal mass. The temperature indoors will remain stable if the doors and windows shut properly and do not let the heat escape that has been generated by the incidence of the sun's rays.

0806 The orientation of this residence benefits natural air conditioning. The desert-facing wall generates a kind of protection from the heat whereas the north-facing façade, located opposite the sea, is the one that has vents to let in the sea breeze to cool the air inside.

0807 In Nordic countries it is convenient to allow the light to enter through the walls, regardless of whether they are north or south-facing. Summers are not as warm as in other latitudes and in winter, when the hours of daylight are significantly reduced, energy savings will be made whenever natural light is used.

0808 The windows and glass walls of the prefabricated Rincon module, developed by the company Marmol Radziner Prefab, have a top layer of insulation and protection from UV rays. The development of materials with these characteristics improves the residents' quality of life.

0809 To increase insulation in this house, enhance thermal protection and reduce the energy costs generated by air conditioning systems, a vacuum has been left between the wooden structure and the outer semi-transparent polycarbonate cladding.

0806

0807

Elevations and floor plans

0808

0809

Bioclimatic diagram

Exploded view

0810 In order to avoid heat loss in windows and glazed walls, there needs to be a thermal break. This involves preventing the inner and outer sides from coming into contact. A divider made of plastic is normally inserted in the aluminum frame forming the window.

0811 To build the roof and outer walls of this property, earth was used from the plot of land itself, which provides excellent insulation. The inside of the building is heated by a simple wood-burning biomass stove.

0812 Apartment buildings can also be sustainable. In this building in Seattle, 60 % of the spaces inside receive natural light, 55 % have natural ventilation and in addition plants are growing in a garden covering 18 % of the roof.

0813 Interstitial condensation, a phenomenon that is caused by the difference in temperature between the surfaces of a material, represents a loss in the insulating capacity of the materials. In this house SIP (Structural Insulated Panels) are used to prevent such loss and improve thermal efficiency.

0814 The diagrams show the difference in solar incidence in winter and summer. Examining the inclination of the roofing and eaves is the best solution for avoiding an excessive amount of sunlight during the hottest months of the year.

0815 If there is a small surface on the roof it may be possible to plant a garden there. The capacity of green roofs to keep the temperature stable inside the building may lead to savings in HVAC costs.

0816 If the house is designed using environmental criteria, it is initially much simpler to orientate it adequately, as is the case here, where the glazed wall, cement flooring and stonework achieve a thermal mass that is used to heat the house in winter.

0817 A good orientation and mounting the house on piers, as is the case of this Australian property, can help to minimize the impact on the environment as a result of erecting a building in a natural setting.

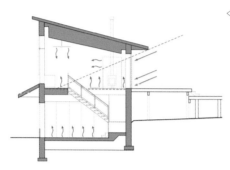

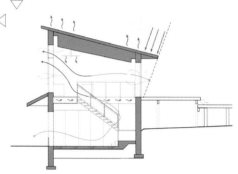

Bioclimatic diagram

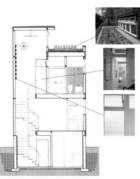

Bioclimatic diagram

0818

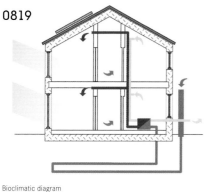

Bioclimatic diagram

0819

0820

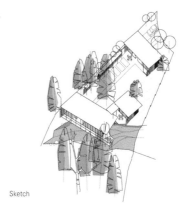

Sketch

0821

Sketch

0818 The glazed facade of this apartment building complies with environmental requirements. Apart from double-glazing, the windows also have a low-emissivity coating and an argon gas airspace between the two layers of glass.

0819 Good ventilation does not necessarily prevent good insulation or the maintenance of a stable temperature inside: to avoid fluctuations in temperature a ventilation system can be installed with a heat recovery facility.

0820 Apart from the layout of the rooms depending on their orientation, the specific location of the house on the site, whether partially embedded or resting on piers, respects the local ecosystem, since it avoids cutting down trees or interrupting the flow of streams, etc.

0821 A bioclimatic house designed with winter in mind should have its main facade oriented in such a way that it receives the most hours of sunlight. This is where the largest windows should be located.

0822

0823

Site plan

0824

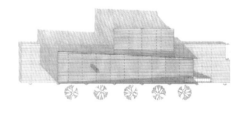

Roof plan

0825

0826

Bioclimatic diagram

0827

0828

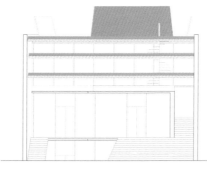

Elevation

0822 If properties are located in a wooded natural environment, the installation of green roofs will help retain the rainwater and provide shelter for birds, insects and microorganisms.

0823 The orientation or specific layout of a property can lead to a more efficient use of the hours of daylight or breezes in the area. Passive air conditioning systems are based on such concepts with a view to reducing energy consumption.

0824 The orientation of the house means that the main facade faces south, receiving the most heat and light. The access to the terrace on the roof is also on the southern side, which is further proof that this layout was not left to chance.

0825 If there is to be an extensive use of glass in the walls of a house, the best thing is to opt for triple-glazed windows and a thermal break, since glass is not in itself a good insulator.

0826 The green roof on this residence in California provides a basis for a small vegetable garden, besides contributing towards the thermal insulation of the inside of the building. Rainwater and recycled graywater are used to water the plants.

0827 Green roofs have several layers. Geotextile protective membranes are placed on the structural base, along with insulation, drainage membranes and a layer of vegetable substratum on which the selected plant species will be embedded.

0828 Even if it is only symbolic, the presence of small areas of plants has a positive effect on the quality of the air, particularly in large cities.

0829

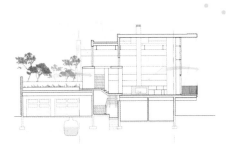

Bioclimatic diagram

0830

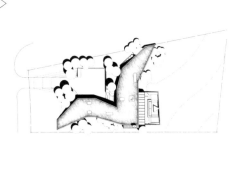

Roof plan

0831

0832

0833

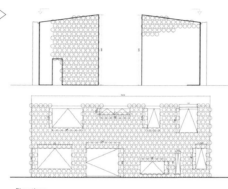

Elevations

0834

0835

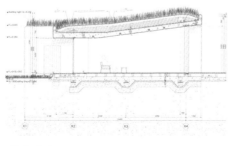

Bioclimatic diagram

0829 If a green roof is installed at an intermediate level in the house, it may help to cool the air before it enters the building. The diagrams of this property show how this idea works: the upper roof is for insulation and the lower one for cooling purposes.

0830 One of the advantages of using green roofs in residences located in the country is their full integration in the landscape, not only for aesthetic reasons, but also because they can adapt to the local climate. This sloping roof, for example, helps protect it from the wind.

0831 To avoid excessive maintenance of green roofs, it is advisable to use native plants, since they are better adapted to the local rainfall.

0832 Another advantage of green roofs, apart from the provision of thermal insulation and rainwater management, is their soundproofing qualities.

0833 Thanks to the hydroponic system, green walls can be installed practically anywhere and can take on some unusual shapes, since the requirements of the vegetable substratum disappear almost entirely.

0834 If constructed properly, a garden roof requires very little maintenance. In this case, the vegetation depends on the seeds brought by the wind and birds in the region.

0835 If there is not much space available or if you want a vertical wall, installing a hydroponic garden is a good option. This system, based on mineral substances, does not require any soil for the plants to grow.

0836 The rainwater is collected by means of gutters and pipes, which take it to the tank. The pipe circuit should be watertight, with it being preferable to store the water in underground tanks to prevent the formation of bacteria and algae.

0837 The house has a sloping roof, with solar PV panels, but a concave angle in the roof collects rainwater for filtering and subsequent reuse. Faucets come with water-saving systems.

0838 Rainwater collection is one of the best ways to save water, since it uses nature's own supply. The collection and pumping system will allow it to be reused in many places around the house.

0839 While it is always cheaper, the use of rainwater can also be of greater or lesser significance depending on the amount of rainfall in the area. In this subtropical region, there is a considerable amount of rainfall, which is stored in a tank located on the roof.

0840 The green roof has a filter system that collects the rainwater which is then reused to water the garden. This is one of the most common uses of rainwater, due to its simple application and because it does not require any special treatment.

0841 The proper slope of the roof and the installation of gutters are the elements that are visible in this property's rainwater collection system, which ends in a tank located underground.

0836

0837

0838
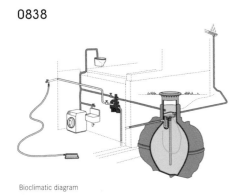

Bioclimatic diagram

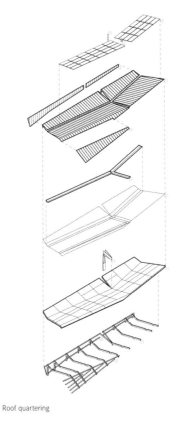

Roof quartering

0839

0840

0841

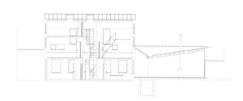

Longitudinal section

0842 Water treatment systems, including those for graywater, may be biological. A sand filtration system, such as the one used in this Australian property, avoids the use of chemicals.

0843 Hand showers are also manufactured with systems that reduce water consumption: they normally mix the air that is swirling around with the incoming water, so that the flow seems to increase even though the amount of water that is consumed is really much lower.

0844 W+W is a proposal from Roca's Innovation Lab that achieves water savings by combining two elements in the bathroom: the washbasin and the toilet. Using the water used in the washbasin for the cistern means a 25% reduction in water consumption.

0845 Saving water is a priority in many countries. The Australian Ian Alexander has designed a bucket that can be adapted to the sink to maximize the use of water for washing the dishes or vegetables. This water can be used in the cistern or the garden depending on how dirty it is.

0846 Graywater comes from the washing machine and the shower and is not normally used as drinking water but reused in situations where there is no need for drinking water: for watering gardens, in washing machines, cisterns, etc.

0842

0843

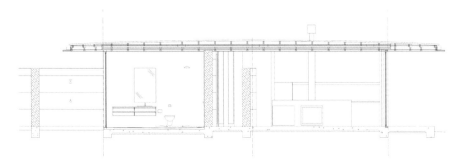

Section

0844

0845

0846

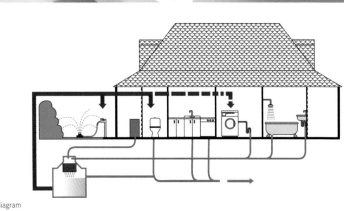

Bioclimatic diagram

0847

0848

0849

0850

0851

0847 To maximize the use of the water resources on this English estate in Suffolk, the rainwater is stored and the drinking water is treated after use so that it can be used to water the plants.

0848 Apart from flow reducers in all the faucets in the house, one of the best ways to reduce water consumption is to replace the baths with showers. This can mean considerable savings at the end of the year.

0849 Another of the most frequent solutions for saving water in the cistern is the use of volumetric reducers, which reduce the gallons of water expelled each time the toilet is flushed. Models such as that of Marcadiferencia can be used, or else bottles filled with sand.

0850 Tres faucets reduce water and energy consumption by 50% thanks to mixer faucets which provide cold water when turned to their central position, and only produce hot water when the lever is moved to the left.

0851 To improve the quality of the graywater and avoid bad smells, it is normal to use settling systems and biological filters before its reuse.

0852 Most modern faucets manufactured nowadays come with flow reducers inside their pipes, thereby combining stylishness with reduced water consumption.

0853 Apart from flow reducers, there are also aerators on the market, which are simple systems that mix air with water. These devices need maintaining to avoid the accumulation of lime, which can make them less efficient.

0854 To save water in bathrooms it is absolutely imperative to install a double push button in the lavatory. There are two types: the one with two flushing cisterns and the one that allows you to stop the toilet flushing whenever you wish.

0855 To reduce water consumption, single mixer faucets can be chosen with flow reducers ready incorporated or with one-click security systems, which require the user to push the switch up if more water is desired.

0856 The best water-saving system would be one with two water mains: one for drinking water, and the other supply for all the other uses, coming from the (previously treated) graywater or rainwater supply.

0857 This other model of faucet has a simple system for saving water: the simple use of a coin to turn the regulating screw underneath the pipe determines the pressure at which the water comes out of the faucet.

0858 There are models of hand showers that incorporate more water-saving devices and health features: the Irisana IR15 model has a ceramic filter, which makes the water release negative ions making the use of soap unnecessary. In addition, it reduces water and energy consumption by as much as 65%.

0859 In cases of properties that are not connected to the sewage system or when water consumption needs to be reduced to the minimum, self-composting toilets can be installed, which work without any water, or models that only use a pint of water each time they are flushed, such as those marketed by Envirolet.

0860 Shower head water stabilizers, which are installed between the faucet and the shower hose, stabilize the flow regardless of how far the faucet is opened.

0861 Placing flow reducers on all the faucets in the house may result in up to a 50% reduction, representing considerable savings in the consumption of drinking water.

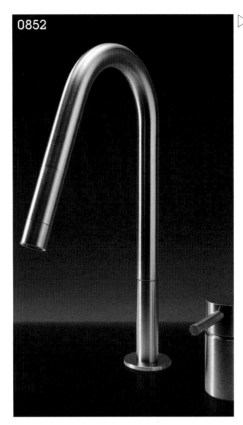

0852

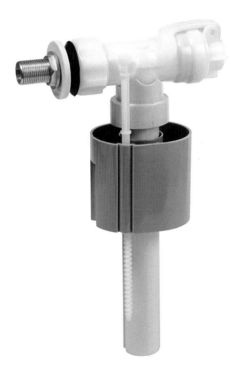

0853

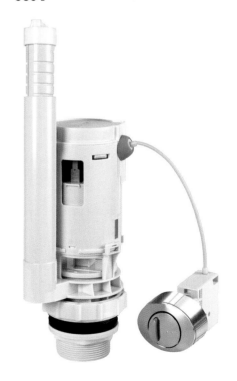

0854

0855

0857

0856

0858

0859

0860

0861

0862 Houses located in natural settings may not be connected to all the mains. In such cases it is a good idea to have tanks to collect rainwater to satisfy most needs that do not require drinking water: cisterns, washing machines, etc.

0863 One of the environmental elements installed in this home designed by Choi Ropiha is a water tank with a capacity to store up to 15,000 liters (just under 4,000 gallons). This tank for collecting rainwater is used together with the reuse of graywater.

0864 Heat and dirt are the main factors that alter the state of the water stored in tanks. Hence it needs to be protected from these two elements. If this is done, the water will not need to be treated so much before it can be reused.

0865 It is essential to slope the roofs, albeit only slightly, so that the rainwater can run into the collectors, located, in this case, at the back of the property.

0866 The water used in this log cabin in Oregon comes from rainwater which is stored in tanks. It is collected in a gutter and transported to an underground earth tube. Some pumps that run on solar energy take it from the earth tube to the tanks and from there into the house.

0867 Metal is the material that is used most often to make tanks to collect water. In this home on Kangaroo Island in Australia, designed by Max Pritchard Architects, the tanks are made of rust-proof galvanized steel.

Bioclimatic diagram

0868

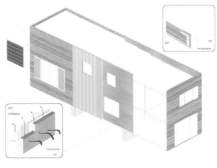

Bioclimatic diagram

0869

0870

0868 Prefab homes, albeit only partially, also bring benefits, such as more lightweight structures, fewer materials and energy savings during construction.

0869 This Santa Monica residence, in Los Angeles, is prefabricated: it was made at the factory with materials that take sustainability criteria into account. On the plot itself it just had to be put together, leading to savings in cost and CO_2 emissions.

0870 Prefabs reduce the cost of building materials and the impact on the environment. In this model structural insulated panels have been used for the floor and ceiling, leading to savings of between 12 and 14% in the amount of energy required for heating and air conditioning.

0871 The manufacture of some of the components and the assembly of all the elements in the factory, including the solar panels, can save time, money and CO_2 emissions in building prefab homes.

0872 These houses, consisting of movable elements and prefabricated parts, are much more flexible in terms of layout than more traditionally built homes.

0873 Nowadays prefab architecture is of excellent quality. This property was constructed with Structural Insulated Panels, which make the manufacturing and building process much cheaper and faster.

0874 The use of cargo containers in prefabricated architecture is a common practice: two of the greatest advantages are the time saved in construction and the greater resilience of the material as opposed to wood or other metallic structures.

0875 To reduce the time taken to erect a building it is better to opt for a prefab. This Swiss residence was built in just four months thanks to its prefabricated wooden structure.

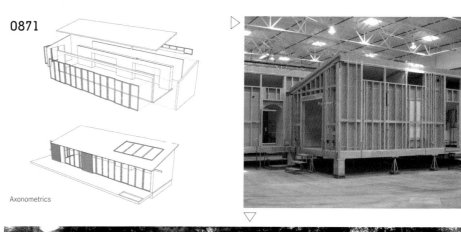

0871

Axonometrics

0872

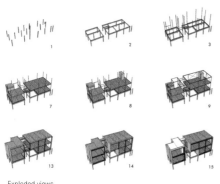

Exploded views

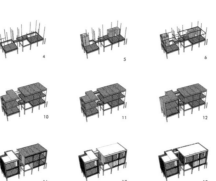

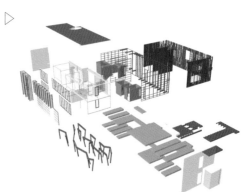

0873

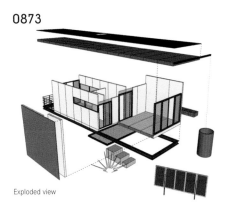

Exploded view

0874

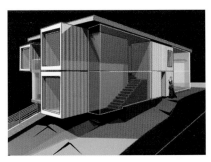

3D Representation

0875

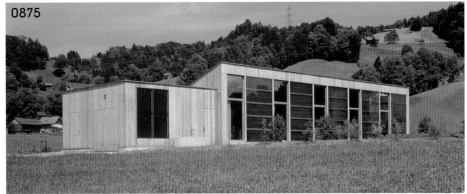

0876 The outer cladding is made of solid, hardwood taken from certified forests in South America, proof that elegance is not incompatible with sustainability.

0877 The use of bamboo as an eco-friendly material is becoming increasingly common. The characteristics of this woody plant, which is extremely pliable, make it suitable for use in construction. Furthermore, thanks to its rapid growth, it is cheaper to cultivate in controlled conditions than other materials like wood.

0878 Using cork on the walls or floors is a good choice as it is excellent for soundproofing and thermal insulation. It is also hard-wearing and resistant to pests.

0879 With respect to sustainability, it is a good idea to demand locally sourced timber, which should come from controlled plantations that guard against deforestation.

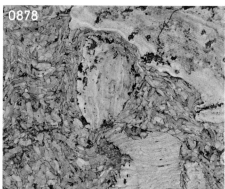

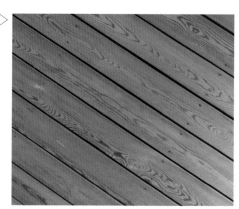

0880

0881

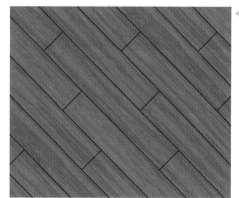

0882

0883

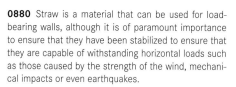

0880 Straw is a material that can be used for load-bearing walls, although it is of paramount importance to ensure that they have been stabilized to ensure that they are capable of withstanding horizontal loads such as those caused by the strength of the wind, mechanical impacts or even earthquakes.

0881 If you want to install bamboo flooring, attention should be paid to the temperature and humidity of the house at the time of assembly, as the planks might dry out.

0882 If desired, natural or non-toxic materials can be used to build a house. To guarantee the source of the wood, for example, it is a good idea to buy FSC-certified wood to make sure that it is not the product of deforestation.

0883 Most of the wood used in the extension for this house comes from a controlled or recycled source. Furthermore, the structure of the mezzanine floor has been left open, thereby avoiding the use of any additional building materials.

0884 The elasticity and strength of bamboo make it suitable for application in railings, shutters, pillars, coverings and cladding.

0885 Timber is considered to be a natural material as, in most cases, it requires very few manufacturing processes to be used in architecture. This characteristic is of course lost where a wood-based product is obtained with huge energy costs or high CO_2 emissions.

0886 Using bamboo as a building material is a good option, provided it is harvested locally from certified plantations and has not been treated with fertilizers or pesticides.

0887

0890

0888

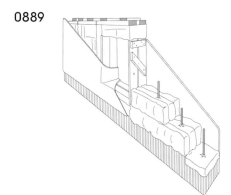

0889

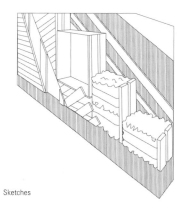

Sketches

0887 To build a house made of straw it is better to enlist the help of a professional, as many aspects of this type of construction, such as the settlement of the bales of straw, cladding, etc are quite complex.

0888 The use of adobe in a house, particularly where the earth from the plot of land is used, is a perfect solution for making savings in building materials and CO_2 derived from the transport and production of other materials.

0889 Apart from material for walls, thanks to its insulating properties, straw can be used to cover roofing and cladding. It is arranged in layers with the rainwater running over the top.

0890 In straw bale construction, two possible methods may be used, or else a hybrid of both: the Nebraska system, which uses the bales as load-bearing walls and structure, or the «post and beam» method, in which the straw is used as a substitute for brick.

0891 For the walls of straw bale houses, a cladding at least 2 cm (0.8 in) thick is recommended to protect the material from damp and the possible attack of rodents.

0892 Healthy, non-toxic materials, such as paints free from solvents and fumes, and wood without formaldehyde, are similar to traditional materials. Hence, their use is not apparent to the eye.

0893 Slate is not recommended for use in paving outdoors in cold climates, since despite being a material that is very solid and resistant to abrasion, it does not tolerate frost very well and it would not take long for the patio flooring to be damaged.

0894 Earth can be used with various methods for building purposes. One of the most common is *rammed earth*, which uses earth from a local source or from the plot itself.

0895 The most eco-friendly way to preserve stonework is to clean it with a Szerelmey liquid solution. A second coating with a calcium silicate primer forms an insoluble layer protecting the stone.

0896 Some of the characteristics of stone might make us choose it for use in our home: durability and low maintenance, good sound-proofing and thermal inertia and efficient protection against the summer heat.

0891

0892

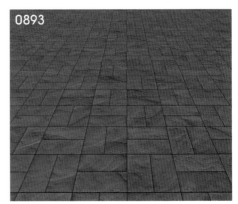

0893

0894

0895

0896

0897 The Swedish design studio Bolon has been working on a new environmental product. A revolutionary plasticizer for floor coverings is presented, under the Bolon® Green initiative, using plant-based raw materials that are 100% renewable.

0898 The covering for this new facade is made of wood certified by the FSC (Forest Stewardship Council), which guarantees the origin of the wood and safeguards forested areas. These walls have enhanced insulation and harness energy use more efficiently.

0899 When building with straw, as with traditional architecture, it is imperative to follow the regulations of each country regarding structures, loads and fire prevention to the letter.

0900 For a healthy home, select materials that do not contain volatile organic compounds or formaldehydes. These are present in paint strippers, adhesives, silicones, etc.

0901

0902

0903

0904

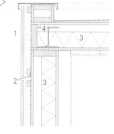

1. Wooden planks (from wasted cable-reels)
2. Water shed (new)
3. Polystyrene insulation (cut out window-pieces out of caravan production process)
4. Steel beams (from washed machine)

0901 The reuse of materials means savings in costs and resources. In this project, wooden planks have been recovered from an old silo, and cleaned and treated for use on the outer deck. The cladding on a barn has also been cleaned and painted for reuse outside.

0902 The cladding on the walls and roof for this house in Canada was achieved with Galvalume, a low-maintenance steel that minimizes solar heat gain, achieving a stable temperature indoors.

0903 Recycled, porcelain ceramic tiles can be used, which have 95% recycled material that is left over from production processes but without losing any of the strength and durability of normal porcelain tiles, such as these Ston-ker Ecologic tiles made by Porcelanosa.

0904 When materials from various origins are reused for architectural purposes their condition and uniformity of size should be taken into account so as to make them easier to use, as in the case of the wooden strips taken from some cable reels, which were reused for the cladding of this house.

0905 Brick walls have a high level of thermal inertia. Hence, they can store the heat radiated onto the outer wall or by the fireplace inside the home, as shown in these photos.

0906 The use of alternative composite or recycled materials is another possibility, providing they are obtained using sustainable methods, and without exhausting the natural resources. Cannabric, a brick derived from industrial hemp (cáñamo), and made by drying in the sun, is a good example.

0907 Reuse may mean using recycled materials, using metals that have been melted down and transformed into new parts, or merely finding a new use for some items, such as the traffic signs that have been converted into fencing and railings in this particular house.

Detail

0908

0909

0910

Axonometric

0911

0908 Recycling materials is essential to avoid generating waste; in this house, for instance, the cladding on the walls was produced from earth taken from the area, while the countertop in the kitchen was made from fragments of recycled glass.

0909 Choosing eco-bricks like those made by Piera will result in significant savings in terms of energy and CO_2 emissions, since alternative heat sources, such as biogas, are used in their production. However, they still look like conventional bricks.

0910 Although it might be laborious, finding building materials in old factories can be a good way to reduce costs. In this case, the steel from a machine in a textile factory was used for the metal frame of the house.

0911 The design and geometrical features of each brick will offer variations in the uses already made of these materials, such as better insulation, greater mechanical strength, etc.

0912 On the top floor of this residence, located south of the city of Lima, in Peru, and overlooking the sea, there is a small pool next to the lounge. The water runs underneath the space and reappears on the other side of the lounge, in the form of a pond.

0913 The fountains and ponds work like sculptural elements and are decisive in defining the style of the garden. In this case, an elongated body of water enhances the zen-like look of the garden.

0914 If you want a spectacular area around the property, it is better to hire a landscape architect. Their knowledge of architecture and gardening will get the most out of the surrounding landscape.

0915 If you want to give the transit areas in a large residential building their own personality, ponds or fountains can be installed. These decorative elements are very effective even if they are quite small in size.

0916 The high water falls, in a cascade, into the swimming pool on the bottom floor, cooling the rooms, lending them an air of privacy, and filtering the light coming in from the north west to make it less harmful. The waterfall effect is made possible thanks to a system of pumps that move the water round the circuit.

0917 Water is an element that makes an infinite number of expressions possible and can be the differentiating factor in a garden lending it its personality. In this case, a simple fountain with five jets starts working its way round a house, making it possible to have a spring garden.

Floor plan

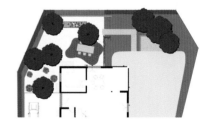

Floor plan

0914

0915

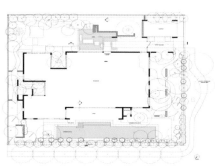

Floor plan

0916

0917

0918 The structure combines teak with stone and concrete, enabling people to move about without coming into contact with the water, although this can be seen from all over the site.

0919 Fountains can function as elements dividing up the space. In this garden, for instance, the fountain and gutter separate the lawn from the area of gravel reserved as a play area for the children.

0920 Ponds, which are also known as reflecting pools, have been constructed inside this house in Costa Rica for various reasons: apart from being a decorative feature that divides the space according to use, they are also used to cool down the inside of the building.

0921 If the gutters carrying the water are incorporated as an integral part of the garden paths, this can have a very original result. Slabs of stone are the best option for crossing over the gutters and fusing land and water together.

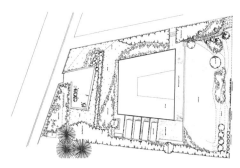

Floor plan

0922 In cold countries, such as Poland, it is a good idea to build indoor pools. In this way, they can be used all year round rather than just in the short summer period. A glass wall will create a connection with the outside.

0923 The design of a swimming pool can make it the feature that ends up defining the look of a property. Infinity pools, for instance, with their simple, elegant lines, are quite common in houses with a contemporary design.

0924 Small plots or non-conventional shapes can also have swimming pools. The solution is to adapt their shape accordingly. In this case, for example, priority has been given to the length of the pool.

0925 The choice of spot for the swimming pool may depend on the planning regulations in place in each area or on the lie of the land. In this case, the architects used the uneven terrain in their project, thereby making it unnecessary to excavate a huge amount of land.

0926 A pond that becomes a pool when it comes outside is the element that defines the interior of this property. This glazed pond-cum-pool separates the kitchen from the lounge and reflects the light, providing indirect lighting for the interior of the property.

0927 In the homes of families with young children it is necessary to take strict safety precautions outside, where the children spend a long time playing. One of the most important of these is to protect the access to the swimming pool, either with traditional metal railings or with safety glass.

0928 Simplicity is the best strategy for a successful swimming pool design, especially if it is embedded in an environment that highlights the landscape or there are spectacular views.

0929 The area around the pool should not be neglected, since this can help create a more relaxing environment. The walls and the stone surrounding this pool are arranged in such a way that, together with the water, they generate a relaxing interplay of planes and cool colors.

0930 Naturalized pools use plants that mimic the function of purifying microorganisms in natural water. The minimum surface for these systems is about 30 sq yard and local species should be chosen to populate it.

0931 An original design for a swimming pool can turn this element, which can often be so uninteresting, into the focal point of the garden. In this case, the pool is elevated above the land so that there is an increased incidence of sunlight on the water and a glazed wall enables you to see what is going on inside.

0932 To make the swimming pool look part of the landscape, it is important to opt for materials that blend in with the house and local surroundings. In this example, polished natural stone has been used in a golden tone for the surround, and turquoise stone for the lining of the pool.

0933 Although having a pool is a huge expense in terms of water, non-aggressive or non-hazardous methods can be used to purify the water, such as the use of salt instead of chlorine in domestic pools.

Floor plan

0929

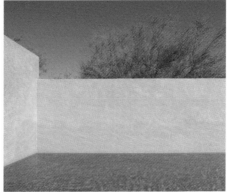

0930

0931

0932

0933

0934

0935

0936

0937

0938

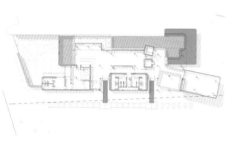

Floor plan

0934 An eco-friendly pool begins with the choice of materials and location. We recommend not making too many changes to the site and using locally sourced stone rather than treated varieties.

0935 Infinity pools are an attractive resource that add another layer of sophistication. In this case, the swimming pool also provides an elegant solution for closing one of the walls and for enhancing its horizontality.

0936 The installation of pergolas or sunshades next to the pool is a solution that will increase the number of hours that can be spent in these places.

0937 An eye-catching solution when the property is vertical or has very little surface area is to incorporate the pool in the design of the house. This strategy requires a technical study to be conducted of the loads that will need to be borne by the structure, but a spectacular result is guaranteed.

0938 To get the most out of it and enhance its presence as a stylish feature forming part of the architectural design, the swimming pool may be located alongside the house or even partially surround it.

0939 It is advisable to decide on the location of the swimming pool when designing the house, since this can determine the shape and layout of the other spaces: main house, annexes, garages, etc.

0940 Privacy in the home is an important issue. One way of increasing it might be to have the swimming pool on the part of the land closest to the densest vegetation.

0939

0940

0941 The choice of materials is crucial for creating a specific atmosphere around the pool and for dividing up the various spaces. In this case, the change of paving has been used to mark off the area of the pool from the porch.

0942 This pool with its pure lines is located in the property's main courtyard, which indicates the importance given to this space by the owners.

0943 It is advisable to reserve a space around swimming pools for activities that are normally carried out in their vicinity: children's games, meals, sunbathing, etc. Wooden flooring and terraces are normally installed for such purposes.

0944 The siting of swimming pools on plots of land depends on the surface available, building codes, and the use you want to give the space. In this case, it has been built next to the main porch, which means it is used more frequently.

0945 Apart from harking back to local tradition, the use of lava stone in the swimming pool at this Hawaiian residence enables the water to be heated thanks to this material's natural uptake of heat from the sun.

0941

Floor plan

0942

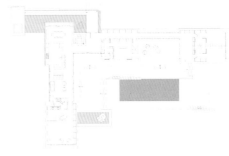

Floor plan

0943

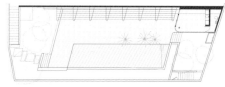

Floor plan

0944

0945

Floor plan

0946

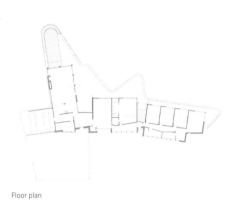

Floor plan

0947

0948

Floor plan

0949

0946 Infinity pools are some of the most popular since they conjure up the feeling of swimming in an area of open water. If, furthermore, they also look out over the landscape, this only heightens the sense of getting away from it all.

0947 Swimming pools can also function as part of the scenery, adding vitality to the surroundings. In this case, the pool surrounds the property and blends in with features of the landscape.

0948 If the pool is located between the various patios outside the house, there is a refreshing effect with a sense of calm. Interconnecting the different areas is a useful tool for energizing the architecture.

0949 Swimming pool designs can enhance the relationship between the architecture and the natural environment. The water here acts as a transition between the house and the Colombian rainforest.

0950

Floor plan

0951

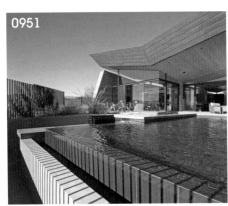

Floor plan

0952

Site plan

0953

0954

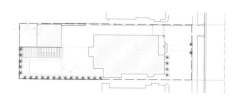

Floor plan

0950 If care is paid to the design and shape of the pool, it can function as a sculptural element reinforcing the personality of a residence and the surrounding area.

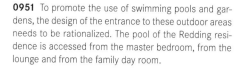

0951 To promote the use of swimming pools and gardens, the design of the entrance to these outdoor areas needs to be rationalized. The pool of the Redding residence is accessed from the master bedroom, from the lounge and from the family day room.

0952 Recycling building materials can also extend to the construction of swimming pools. Tanks from an old industry have been put to an original use here: they now form the swimming pool and hot tub.

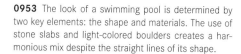

0953 The look of a swimming pool is determined by two key elements: the shape and materials. The use of stone slabs and light-colored boulders creates a harmonious mix despite the straight lines of its shape.

0955

0954 One of the most important aspects of designing swimming pools concerns the type of material that will be used to surround it. This should be resilient and non-slip.

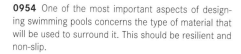

0955 The orientation of the swimming pool towards the landscape has inspired the architects to install glass in one of the walls and thus eliminate the boundaries blocking the views from the water.

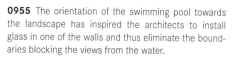

0956 Having a spa at home is as easy as installing a hot tub in the bathroom instead of a conventional bath. They are not too complicated to install and current prices are not as prohibitive as they used to be.

0957 The place housing the indoor pool has been converted into a space for relaxation: the waterfall energizing the area and the jacuzzi blend in with the views of the garden and are a good place to unwind.

0958 When reserving a space to relax and pamper yourself, you should consider the installations and space that will be occupied by the machinery, whether you intend to have a sauna or a hydromassage shower cabin, to ensure that the end result is a spacious, relaxed atmosphere.

0959 If you want to add a bit of comfort in the property's water area, reserving part of the surface of the pool to install a jacuzzi is a good option.

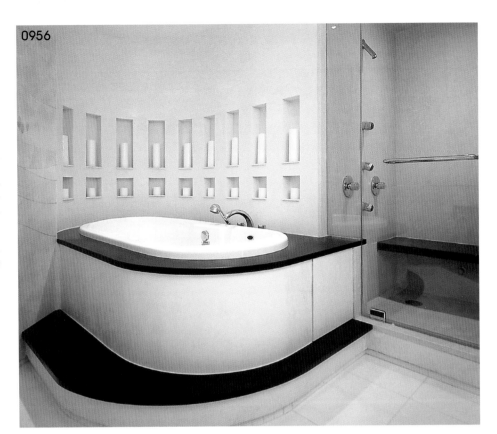

0960 A Japanese soaking tub (ofuro), used to purify body and soul, is very easy to install in the home. All that is needed is the space for the tub with hot water and a relaxing atmosphere.

0961 The chance to integrate a space in the surrounding landscape should not be overlooked, particularly when this is a feature that can be used to enhance the atmosphere of the place.

0962 Lighting up the pool and jacuzzi at night is a plus for the house as, apart from being the best solution for prolonging the number of hours they are used, it is also a safety aspect that should be taken into consideration by families with young children.

0963 If the layout of the house is re-organized, it may be possible to find a spot for an indoor *spa*. In this case, the garage has been converted into a fitness room with a swimming pool and sauna included.

0964

0965

0966

0967

0968

0969

0964 Even though they may go unnoticed, it is vital that wastepipes be installed correctly for the bath to work properly and to guard against bad odor and stop the pipes clogging up.

0965 Outdoor installations, which are more attractive and stylish, need to be positioned with great care, and therefore we recommend hiring professionals with expert knowledge of more complex installations.

0966 The shower installed in these bathrooms in the Megius property has LED lighting fixtures. This combination offers a shower with the effect of rain, enhanced by color therapy. These devices regulate water and light consumption, thereby offering increased comfort in the shower without squandering resources.

0967 If power shower columns are to be installed or models incorporating water massage systems, it is worth knowing that these elements require greater pressure and a larger quantity of water.

0968 The bathroom fittings shown here are small and simple in design, with a matte finish, to emphasize the minimalist, ethereal look of the bathroom. Another model in the same series has been installed in the shower.

0969 If you decide to install wall-mounted bidets or toilets, the weight of the ceramic pan needs to be taken into account, along with the additional anchorage points for it to be fixed in place properly and the capacity of the wall to bear the weight.

0970 A strategically placed white wall can function as a projector screen. In this way, a living room or bedroom can quickly become a room where you enjoy a movie or a video game without the need for large installations.

0971 These devices designed by Marcel Wanders help towards responsible energy consumption within the household. By monitoring the electricity usage at all times they inform users and help reduce consumption and wattage.

0972 When choosing a home cinema system it should be simple to use and have all the functions required. There are sophisticated systems with touch screen for player control, monitor, speakers and other controlgear.

0973 A projector installed in the courtyard of the main home projects movies on the façade of the guest annex. Total interaction between the audiovisual technology, projector, the architectural design of house and the screen is achieved.

0974 The use of projectors has become more widespread, as they bring together the functions of several technologies. Everything is done via the computer and it is not necessary to duplicate devices that can perform the same functions: TV, movie player, stereo, etc.

0975 To avoid disrupting the aesthetics of the interiors, opt for audio-visual equipment or computers that are integrated, either by color or material, or other small-scale equipment but with proven efficiency.

0976 Current technology offers multiple opportunities to enjoy television such as simultaneous programs or distribute the image across multiple screens.

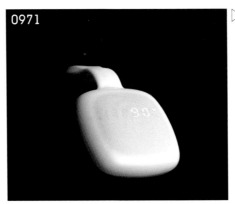
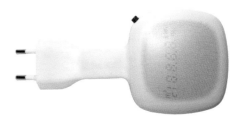

0973

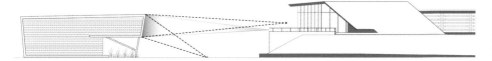

Diagram

0974

0975

0976

0977

0978

0979

0980

0981

0982

0983

0977 If audiovisual equipment is of high quality, the room should have adequate acoustics, otherwise you would not enjoy the full potential they offer.

0978 In open-plan homes like lofts, it is easier to change the layout of furniture and transform a living room into a music room for leisure times.

0979 If you do not want entertainment devices to be visible in the interior, there are several options: some stores, such as Artcoustic, design speakers with interchangeable screens that can be stamped with your chosen picture or design.

0980 If you have enough space, gamers can install a real games room at home: pull-down screen, projector, surround sound and a chair with steering wheel simulator.

0981 Projectors are small mobile elements that can be moved inside the house and therefore can transform any corner into a makeshift movie theater.

0982 In addition to the plasma screen, have another screen if you want to show movies in a larger format, as they roll up, they do not affect the configuration of the space.

0983 Installing a stereo or TV in the bedroom is a good option if you want to enjoy more intimate moments, especially when you have a large family.

0684 It is increasingly more common to have a room equipped for new technologies: computers, projectors, music systems, etc. In this way the "media" activity is concentrated in one room without disturbing people who are in other spaces.

0985 The proliferation of wireless Internet connection and the increasingly common use of laptops and tablets can turn any corner of the house in a study.

0986 It is no wonder that Japan, a country with great technological development is one of the places where automation is most widely implemented. For increased comfort at home, incorporate Japanese toilets, which regulate water flow, temperature, etc.

0987 For years home automation has made life easier inside houses and the temperature, the height of the blinds, sound systems, etc can be remotely controlled from any room.

0988 Technology should only be incorporated into the home to facilitate day to day activities and to enjoy life more at home. The installation of showers with chromotherapy provides wellbeing and is not expensive.

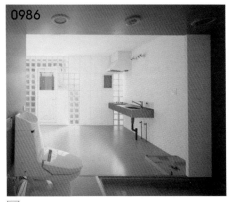

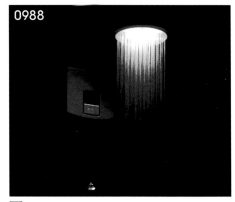

0989

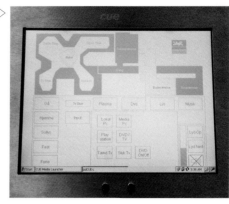

0990

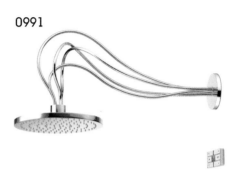

0991

0992

0989 The rotating central column of this apartment includes a number of technological devices for communication, information, entertainment and control.

0990 One of the advantages of motorized systems is that you can install large architectural elements, such as this divider panel that emerges from the floor that could not otherwise be installed.

0991 One of the places where automation has most been developed is in the bathroom. Thus, it is common to find built-in radios, tactile devices that control the temperature and the force of water, timers, etc.

0992 The option to install a mechanical system in the furniture of this small studio multiplies the use of the spaces. When the dining table is not needed, for example, it is concealed in the floor and more space is created in the living room.

0993 In the refurbishment of this Victorian house a large glass façade has been installed that works as the sash windows typical of such homes. The large glass panels, measuring 6.4 x 4 m (21 x 13 ft), meant that a motor had to be installed to move them.

0994 All mobile parts of this home near Warsaw move using a motorized system. These mechanisms have gradually developed increasingly complex functions to facilitate the life of the occupants and add value to their homes.

0995 The living room of this home opens onto the exterior through a large glass door. The motorized system vertically moves the glass surface and keeps it elevated.

0996 These large panels that act as shutters and roof eaves, have a pneumatic system to move and lift them more quickly, easily and safely.

0997

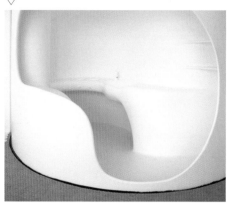

0998

0999

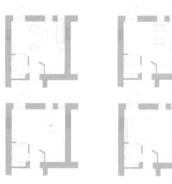

Floor plans

1000

0997 Prefabricated homes often incorporate new technologies. This original studio has a motor that generates the rotation of a space that integrates three rooms: kitchen, bedroom and bathroom.

0998 Not all mechanical systems must necessarily work with electricity. This pulley system that moves the panels enclosing the home is operated with a handle.

0999 Hydraulic systems are one of the best mechanical inside the homes; they allow the precise control of movements in spite of their great strength.

1000 Motorized systems have represented a breakthrough in interior design, especially in small spaces. They are also useful, as in this case, to emphasize the minimalist style of an apartment.

0001, 0251
Hobby A., Schuster & Maul, Gerold Peham/Nomad Home
www.nomadhome.com
© Marc Haader (0001)
© Nomad Home ® Trading GesmbH (0251)
0002, 0058, 0369
Kerry Joyce Associates
www.kerryjoyce.com
© Dominique Vorillon
0003, 0224
Tom Allisma
http://tomallismaproductions.com
© Tom Kessler
0004, 0062
Leonardo Annecca/L-A-Design
www.l-a-design.com
© Miaz Brothers, Michael Greag
0005
Alchemy Architects
www.alchemyarchitects.com
© Alchemy Architects
0006, 0363
Mandi Rafaty/Tag Front
www.tagfront.com
© Dean Pappas/Tag Front
0007
Studio Aisslinger
www.aisslinger.de
© Steffen Jänicke & Jens Vogt
0008, 0095
Silvestrin Salmaso Architects
www.claudiosilvestringiulianasalmaso.com
© dieterphotodesigner.de
0009, 0624
Pablo Uribe
www.studiouribe.com
© Claudia Uribe
0010
MACK Architect(s)
www.markmack.com
© Takashi Hatekeyama
0011
Spoerri Thommen Architekten
www.spoerrithommen.ch
© Michael Freisager Fotografie
0012, 0066, 0104, 0208, 0674
AvroKO
www.avroko.com
© Michael Webber (0012, 0208)
© Michael Weber, Yuki Kuwana (0066, 0104, 0674)
0013, 0057, 0263, 0302, 0350, 0374, 0543, 0613
Ptang Studio (0013, 0057, 0350, 0374)
Philip Tang, Brian Ip, Joanne Lau/Ptang Studio (0263, 0543)
Philip Tang, Brian Ip, Harvey Tsang, Joanne Lau/Ptang Studio (0302)
www.ptangstudio.com
© Ulso Tang (0013, 0057, 0263, 0350, 0543)
© Philip Tang (0302, 0374, 0613)
0014, 0737, 0816, 0822
Altius Architecture Inc & Sustain Design Studio (0014)
Altius Architecture (0737, 0816, 0822)
http://altius.net
© Altius Architecture Inc & Sustain Design Studio
© Altius Architecture (0737, 0816, 0822)
0015
Avi Laiser & Amir Shwarz
www.al-arch.com
© Miri Davidovitch
0016, 0027, 0079, 0323, 0580
The Apartment Creative Agency
http://www.theapt.com
© Michael Weber

0017, 0283, 0321, 0518
Autoban Office
http://autoban212.com
© Levent Bozkurt (0017)
© Ali Bekman (0283, 0321, 0518)
0018, 0317, 0632
Griffin Enright Architects
www.griffinenrightarchitects.com
© Benny Chan, Fotoworks
0019
Joey Ho Design
www.joeyhodesign.com
© Graham Ude, Ray Lau
0020, 0708
Caramel Architekten
www.caramel.at
© Caramel Architekten (0020)
© Johannes Felsch, Caramel Architekten (0708)
0021, 0340, 0812, 0818
Mithun
http://mithun.com
© Bemjamin Benschneider, Juan Fernández
0022
Atelier A5
www.a-a5.com
© Sadahiro Shimizu/Atelier A5
0023, 0135, 0356, 0416, 0594
Christian Heiss, Michael Thomas, Thomas Mayer/Atelier HEISS
www.atelier-heiss.at
© Peter Burgstaller/Archv Atelier Heiss
0024, 0507, 0515, 0533
Vicente Wolf and Associate David Rogal
www.vicentewolf.com
© Vicente Wolf
0025
Gus Wüstemann
www.guswustemann.com
© Gus Wüstemann
0026, 0315, 0420
Barton Myers Associates
www.bartonmyers.com
© Jim Simmons
0027 (0016)
0028, 0874
DeMaria Design Associates
http://demariadesign.com
© Andre Movsesyan, Christian Kienapfel
0029, 0229
Stanic Harding
www.stanicharding.com
© Paul Gosney
0030, 0193, 0234, 0284, 0379, 0502, 0669, 0968
Hofman Dujardin Architecten
www.hofmandujardin.nl
© Matthijs van Roon
0031, 0298
Guillermo Arias and Luis Cuartas (0031)
Luis Cuartas (0298)
www.octubre.com.co
© Eduardo Consuegra, Pablo Rojas, Álvaro Gutiérrez (0031)
© Eduardo Consuegra (0298)
0032, 0085, 0100
Yann CHU/Atelier Marais Design
+886 2 8787 4097
© Marc Gerritsen
0033, 0600, 0694
Architects EAT
www.eatas.com.au
© Shania Shegedyn, John Gollings, Jason Reekie (0033, 0600)
© Craig Shell, Rhiannon Slatter (0694)
0034, 0268, 0359, 0733, 0877
RES 4 Architecture
http://re4a.com
© RES 4 Architecture

0035, 0044
Juan Carlos Doblado
www.juancarlosdoblado.com
© Alex Kornhuber (0035)
© Elsa Ramírez (0044)
0036, 0309
Naoki Terada/Terada Design Architects
www.teradadesign.com
© Yuki Omori
0037, 0265, 0631
A-Cero
www.a-cero.com
© Santiago Barrio (0037, 0631)
© Alberto Peris Caminero (0265)
0038, 0191, 0241, 0243, 0339
Agustí Costa Estudi de Disseny
www.agusticosta.com
© David Cardelús
0039, 0204, 0534, 0544, 0555, 0564, 0576
Matali Crasset (0039, 0534, 0544, 0555)
Matali Crasset, Marco Salgado, Francis Fichot (0204, 0576)
www.matalicrasset.com
© Matali Crasset Productions (0039, 0534, 0544, 0555, 0564)
© Patrick Gries (0204, 0576)
0040
XTEN Architecture
http://xtenarchitecture.com
© Art Gray
0041, 0046
Martin Schneider Architeckten
www.ms-arc.de
© Cornelis Gollhardt
0042, 0054, 0315, 0331
Felipe Assadi & Francisca Pulido
www.assadi.cl
© Guy Wenborne
0043, 0207, 0601
Lichtblau.wagner Architekten
www.lichtblauwagner.com
© Bruno Klomfar
0044 (0035)
0045, 0377, 0863
Choi Ropiha
http://chrofi.com
© Simon Whitbred, Brett Boardman
© Brett Boardman (0863)
0046 (0041)
0047, 0065, 0300, 0514, 0526, 0528, 0530, 0585, 0588, 0638, 0966
Filippo Bombace
www.filippobombace.com
© Luigi Filetici (0047, 0065, 0300, 0526, 0528, 0530, 0585)
© Anna Galante (0514, 0588, 0638, 0966)
0048, 0195, 0296, 0646
Philippe Harden, Atelier 9 Portes
www.philippeharden.com
© Philippe Harden
0049
Sami Rintala
www.rintalaeggertsson.com
© Sami Rintala
0050, 0482
Michael Meredith, Hilary Sample/MOS
www.mos-office.net
© Florian Holzherr
0051
Armel Néouze
http://d3architectes.fr
© Armel Néouze
0052, 0428, 0995
Taylor Smyth Architects
www.taylorsmyth.com
© Taylor Smyth Architects (0052)
© Ben Rahn/ A-Frame (0428, 0995)

0053 (0355)
Kiyonobu Nakagame & Associates
www.nakagame.com
© K. Torimura, N. Meguro
0054 (0042)
0055 (0035)
HŠH Architekti
www.hsharchitekti.cz
© Ester Havlová
0056 (0346)
MAD Moehrleinvandelft architekten
www.madarchitekten.nl
© Twan de Veer
0057 (0013)
0058 (0002)
0059 (0306), 0212
Jeff Etelamaki Design Studio
www.je-designstudio.com
© Steve Williams
0060, 0152, 0154, 0162, 0930, 0994
Robert Konieczny, Marlena Wolnik / KWK Promes (0060, 0152, 0162, 0930)
Robert Konieczny / KWK Promes (0154)
www.kwkpromes.pl
© KWK PROMES (0060, 0152, 0162, 0930, 0994)
© Juliusz Sokolowski, Aleksander Rutkowski (0154)
0061, 0365, 0412
Dawson Brown Architecture
N.A.
© Anthony Browell, Patrick Bingham Hall
0062 (0004)
0063, 0299
Dietrich Schwartz
www.schwarz-architekten.com
© Frédérik Comtesse
0064, 0247, 0249, 0766
i29 interior architects
www.i29.nl
© i29 interior architects
0065 (0047)
0066 (0012)
0067, 0358
Esther Hagenlocher, Sabine Storp, Patrick Weber
www.s-w-arch.com
© Nina Siber
0068, 0536, 0567
Target Living
www.targetliving.com
© Philip Vile
0069, 0276, 0368, 0577, 0641, 0667, 0668
MoHen Design International
www.mohen-design.com
© MoHen Design International (0069, 0276, 0368, 0577, 0641, 0667)
© Maoder Chou (0668)
0070, 0250, 0267, 0274, 0289, 0295, 0304, 0313, 0324, 0529
One Plus Partnership
www.onepluspartnership.com
© Gabriel Leung (0070, 0250, 0267, 0274)
© Ajax Law Ling Kit (0289)
© Ajax Law Ling Kit, Virginia Lung (0295, 0304)
© Virginia Lung (0313, 0324, 0529)
0071, 0460
Hiromasa Mori & Tayuka Hosokai
http://takuyahosokai.com
© 1980
0072 (0173), 0089, 0286, 0308, 0513, 0621
CJ Studio (0072, 0286, 0308, 0513)
Shi-Chieh Lu Studio (0089)
www.shi-chieh-lu.com
© Kuomin Lee (0089)
© Marc Gerritsen (0072, 0286, 0308, 0513, 0621)

0073, 0118
Christian Leibenger con Laida Memba, Xavi Rodríguez, Mattia Sartori / Salero
N.A.
© Pol Cucala
0074, 0512
Studio Damilano
www.damilanostudio.com
© Michele da Vita
0075
SchappacherWhite Ltd.
http://schappacherwhite.com
© SchappacherWhite Ltd.
0076, 0133, 0307, 0402
Olavi Koponen
olli.koponen@kolumbus.fi
© Jussi Tianen
0077, 0109
Brunete Fraccaroli
www.brunetefraccaroli.com.br
© Tuca Reinés (0077)
© Joao Ribeiro (0109)
0078 (0303)
Staughton Architects
www.starch.com.au
© Shannon McGrath
0079 (0016)
0080, 0151, 0216, 0221, 0342
Architectural Studio Simone Micheli
www.simonemicheli.com
© S.M.A.H. (0080, 0151)
© Mario Corsini / ASA 64 (0216)
© Vincenzo Milione (0221, 0342)
0081
Knott Architects
www.knottarchitects.co.uk
© Knott Architects
0082, 0101, 0259, 0399, 0547, 0618
www.maynardarchitects.com
Andrew Maynard Architects
© Kevin Hui (0082, 0101, 0259, 0399, 0618)
© Peter Bennetts, Dan Mahon (0547)
0083
Kazuhiko Oishi
oishi.architect@jcom.home.ne.jp
© Koiji Okamoto
0084
Ten Arquitectos
www.ten-arquitectos.com
© Jaime Navarro
0085 (0032)
0086
Marcio Kogan
www.marciokogan.com.br
© Arnaldo Pappalardo
0087, 0451, 0920
Min | Day
www.minday.com
© Larry Gawel (0087, 0451)
© Min | Day (0920)
0088, 0735, 0742
ZeroEnergyDesign
www.zeroenergydesign.com
© ZeroEnergyDesign
0089 (0072)
0090, 0199, 0227, 0386, 0772
Jarmund Vigsnæs AS Architects MNAL
www.jva.no
© Ivan Brodey (0090, 0227, 0386)
© Nils Petter Dale (0199, 0772)
0091, 0114
Manuel Serrano Arquitectos
http://serrano-arquitectos.net
© J. Latova

0092, 0343
Kyu Sung Woo Architects
www.kswa.com
© KSWA
0093, 0121, 0225, 0598
Paskin Kyriakides Sands Architects
www.pksarchitects.com
© Paskin Kyriakides Sands Architects
0094
Eldridge Smerin
www.eldridgesmerin.com
© Lyndon Douglas
0095 (0008)
0096, 0112, 0539
Double G
www.doubleg.fr
© André Thoraval
0097, 0730
Peter Hájek Architekti
www.hajekarchitekti.cz
© Ester Havlova
0098, 0904, 0910
2012Architecten
http://2012architecten.nl
© Allard van der Hoeck
0099, 0137
Pitman Tozer Architects
www.pitmantozer.com
© Nick Kane
0100 (0032)
0101 (0082)
0102, 0353
FORMA Design
http://formaonline.com
© Goeffrey Hodgson
0103
Form Design Architecture
www.form-architecture.co.uk
© Mathew Weinreb
0104 (0012)
0105
SCDA Architects
www.scdaarchitects.com
© Peter Mealin / Jacob Termansen
0106, 0630
Toshimitsu Kuno, Nobuki Nomura / Tele-Design (0106)
Chikara Matsuba / Tele-Design (0630)
www.tele-design.jp
© Tatsuya Naoki, Tamotsu Matsumoto (0106)
© Ryota Atarashi (0630)
0107, 0736
Rongen Architekten
www.rongen-architekten.de
© Rongen Architekten
0108 (0345)
West Architecture
www.westarchitecture.co.uk
© Peter Cook
0109 (0077)
0110, 0156, 0607, 0620, 0643, 0756, 0981
UdA
www.uda.it
© Emilio Conti (0110)
© Carola Ripamonti (0077, 0756)
© Alberto Ferrero (0607)
© Heiko Semeyer (0620, 0643)
© Grazia Blanco / Ike Branco Productions (0981)
0111, 0219, 0330, 0461
Aidlin Darling Design
www.aidlindarlingdesign.com
© Matthew Millman (0111)
© Sharon Risendorph (0219, 0461)
© John Sutton (0330)
0112 (0096)

0113, 0253
Architecture Republic
www.architecture-republic.com
© Paul Tierney Photography
0114 (0091)
0115, 0213
Plystudio
www.ply-studio.com
© Stzernstudio
0116
Michel Rojkind + Simon Hamui
www.rojkindarquitectos.com
© Jaime Navarro
0117
Hiroaki Ohtani
ohtani@dss.nifs.ac.jp
© Kouji Okamoto
0118 (0073)
0119, 0738, 0841
Marc Opdebeeck
www.modelmo.be
© Marie-Hélène Grégoire, Jacky Delorme
0120, 0986
Atelier Tekuto
www.tekuto.com
© Makoto Yoshida
0121 (0093)
0122, 0278, 0591, 0970
Carlo Ratti Associati
www.carloratti.com
© Pino dell'Aquila, Walter Nicolino, Max Tomasinelli (0122, 0591, 0970)
© Pino dell'Aquila, Walter Nicolino (0278)
0123
Valerio Dewalt Train Associates
www.buildordie.com
© Barbara Karant
0124, 0472, 0622
Darren Petrucci
http://a-i-rinc.com
© Bill Timmerman
0125, 0329, 0334, 0921
Ibarra Rosano Design
www.ibarrarosano.com
© Bill Timmerman
0126, 0174, 0325, 0626, 0792
Bercy Chen Studio
http://bcarc.com
© Mike Osborne, Joseph Pettyjohn (0126, 0174, 0792)
© Ryan Michael, Joseph Pettyjohn (0325, 0626)
0127, 0226
Fernandes & Capanema
http://fernandescapanema.com.br
© Fernandes & Capanema (0127)
© Marri Nogueira, Clausem Bonifacio (0226)
0128, 0344, 0516
CL3 Architects
www.cl3.com
© Eddie Siu (0128, 0516)
© Nirut Benjabanpot (0344)
0129
Keizou Matsuda
+81 726010 0895
© Keizou Matsuda
0130, 0232, 0360
Eric Cobb Architects
www.cobbarch.com
© Steve Keating, Eric Cobb
0131, 0380, 0553
Camilla Benedini
http://benedinipartners.it
© Alessandro Anselmi

0132, 0653, 0658
Stadler + Partner
www.planungswelt.de
© Uli Gohs
0133 (0076)
0134, 0230, 0319, 0349, 0436, 0701
Paul McAneary Architects (0134)
Paul McAneary, Alexandra Toogood/Paul McAneary Architects (0230, 0436)
Paul McAneary, Mattias Laumayer/Paul McAneary Architects (0319, 0349, 0701)
www.paulmcaneary.com
© Paul McAneary Architects
0135 (0023)
0136, 0367, 0550
Leone Design Studio
www.royleone.com
© Steve Williams (0136)
© Mikiko Kikuyama (0367, 0550)
0137 (0099)
0138, 0338, 0395
UCArchitect
www.ucarchitect.ca
© UCArchitect
0139, 0287
Wood Marsh Architecture
www.woodmarsh.com.au
© Peter Bennetts
0140, 0698, 0826
Bricault Design
http://bricault.ca
© Kenji Arai (0140, 0698)
© Richard Grigsby, Kenji Arai (0826)
0141, 0190, 0197, 0211
mOrq Architecture
www.morq.it
© Aliocha Merker
0142, 0811, 0834
Hiroshi Nakamura & NAP Architects
www.nakam.info
© Daici Ano (0083)
© NAP Architects (0811, 0834)
0143
Dekleva Gregoric
www.dekleva-gregoric.com
© Matevz Paternoster
0144, 0288
Martin Rauch, Boltshauser Architekten
www.boltshauser.info
© Beat Bühler
0145
Blank Studio
www.blankspaces.net
© Bill Timmerman
0146, 0806
Nasser Abulhasan, Joaquín Pérez Goicoechea/AGI Architects
www.agi-architects.com
© AGI Architects, Nelson Garrido
0147, 0239, 0346, 0382, 0697, 0941
Michael P. Johnson Design Studios
www.mpjstudio.com
© Bill Timmerman
0148, 0604
Anabela Leitão, Daiji Kondo/A-LDK
anabela.leitao@mail.telepac.pt
daiji.kondo@mail.telepac.pt
© Daiji Kondo
0149
Hirotaka Satoh
www.synapse-net.jp
© Hirotaka Satoh
© Aliocha Merker

0150, 0177, 0182, 0183, 0185, 0238
Gary Chang, Andrew Holt, Howard Chang, Popeye Tsang, Yee Lee/EDGE Design Intitute (0150, 0182, 0183, 0185, 0238)
Gary Chang, Raymond Chan/EDGE Design Institute (0177)
www.edge.hk.com
© Asawaka Satoshi, Liu Ruilin, Howard Chang, Gary Chang (0150)
© EDGE Design Institute (0177, 0182, 0185, 0238)
© Almond Chu (0183)
0151 (0080)
0152 (0060)
0153, 0189, 0306, 0699, 0794
Jesse Bornstein, Myung Jong Lee/Bornarch (0153, 0189, 0306, 0699)
Jesse Bornstein/Bornarch (0794)
www.bornarch.com
© Bernard Wolf, Tom Bonner (0153, 0306)
© Bernard Wolf (0189, 0699, 0794)
0154 (0060)
0155, 0443, 0603, 0702
Mark Dziewulski
www.dzarchitect.com
© Keith Cronin
0156 (0110)
0157, 0785, 0892
Rockhill + Associates
www.rockhillandassociates.com
© Dan Rockhill
0158, 0364, 0602, 0774, 0793
CCS Architecture (0158, 0602, 0690, 0774)
Cass Smith, Sean Kennedy/CCS Architecture (0364, 0793)
www.ccs-architecture.com
© Matthew Millman (0158, 0602, 0774)
© Brendan P Macrae, Prime Lens Photography (0364, 0793)
© Javier Haddad Conde/CCS Architecture (0690)
0159, 0625, 0662
Nicolas Gwenael/Curiosity
www.curiosity.jp
© Daici Ano
0160, 0440, 0931
Eric Rosen Architects
www.ericrosen.com
© Erich Koyama
0161, 0200, 0459
Kevin Defreitas Architects
http://defreitasarchitects.com
© Harrison Photographic
0162 (0060)
0163, 0255
Anna Nakamura + Taiyo Jinno/EASTERN design office
www.eastern.e-arc.jp
© Kouichi Torimura
0164
Casey Brown Architecture
www.caseybrown.com.au
© Rob Brown
0165, 0273, 0455, 0894, 0951
Kendle Design Collaborative
www.kendledesign.com
© Rick Brazil, Prescott, AZ
0166, 0554
WORKac
www.work.ac
© Adam Friedberg
0167, 0562, 0660, 0663
Anthony Chan/Cream
www.cream.com.hk
© CREAM (0167, 0663)
© Virgile Simon Bertrand (0562, 0660)
0168, 0272, 0954, 0959
Abramson Teiger Architects
www.abramsonteiger.com
© Richard Barnes (0168, 0272)
© John Linden (0954, 0959)

0257 (0186)
0258, 0722
Markus Wespi Jérôme de Meuron Architekten
www.wespidemeuron.ch
© Hannes Henz
0259 (0082)
0260, 0897
Bolon
www.bolon.com
© Bolon
0261
Gil Percal
www.gil-percal.com
© Gilles Gustève
0262, 0605, 0692, 0718
Paul Cha (0605, 0692, 0718)
Cha & Innerhofer Architects (0262)
www.paulchaarchitect.com
© Dao-Lou Z
0263 (0013)
0264
©6 Architecture
www.at-six.com
© Adrian Gregorutti
0265 (0037)
0266
Jean-Marie Massaud for Axor
www.massaud.com
© Axor
0267 (0070)
0268 (0034)
0269, 0326
Frank La Rivière
www.frank-la-riviere.com
© Ryota Atarashi/FrankLa Rivière/Shinkenchiku-sha
0270, 0291, 0869, 0873
Office of Mobile Design by Jennifer Siegal, M.P. Johnson Design
Studio (0270)
Office of Mobile Design by Jennifer Siegal (0291, 0869)
Office of Mobile Design by Jennifer Siegal, TaliesinDesign/Suild
Studio, M.P. Johnson Design Studio (0873)
www.designmobile.com
© Bill Timmerman (0270, 0873)
© Laura Hull (0291, 0869)
0271, 0303, 0354
Turnbull Griffin Haesloop
tgharchitects.com
© David Wakely
0272 (0168)
0273 (0165)
0274 (0070)
0275 (0256)
0276 (0069)
0277, 0336, 0362, 0448, 0477, 0612, 0791, 0945, 0973
Belzberg Architects
www.belzbergarchitects.com
© Art Gray Photography (0277, 0477, 0612)
© Benny Chan Fotoworks (0362, 0791, 0973, 0336)
© Benny Chan Fotoworks, Belzberg Architects (0448, 0945)
0278 (0122)
0279
Takao Shiotsuka Atelier
www.shio-atl.com
© Kaori Ichikawa
0280 (0188)
0281, 0335, 0617
Pablo Fernández Lorenzo, Pablo Redondo Díez
www.arquipablos.com
© Pablo Fernández Lorenzo
0282, 0484
Felipe del Río, Federico Campino/OPA
www.opa.cl
© Nico Saieh

0283 (0017)
0284 (0030)
0285, 0480
Emilio Llobat Guarino/Maqla Adiu
www.maqla.com
© Emilio Llobat Guarino
0286 (0072)
0287 (0139)
0288 (0144)
0289 (0070)
0290, 0538
Wary Meyers Decorative Arts
www.warymeyers.com
© John Meyers
0291 (0270)
0292, 0786, 0998
Olson Kundig Architects
www.olsonkundigarchitects.com
© Benjamin Benschneider (0292)
© Jim Bartsch, Tim Bies, Nikolas Koenig (0786)
© Undine Pröhl (0998)
0293 (0256)
0294 (0248)
0295 (0070)
0296 (0048)
0297
André Putman
www.studioputman.com
© Courtesy of Bisazza
0298 (0031)
0299 (0063)
0300 (0047)
0301
Non Kitsch Group
N.A.
© Jan Verlinde
0302 (0013)
0303 (0271)
0304 (0070)
0305
Gray Organschi Architecture
http://grayorganschi.com
© Bo Crocket
0306 (0153)
0307 (0076)
0308 (0072)
0309 (0036)
0310, 0361, 0401, 0587
Zen Architects
www.zenarchitects.com
© Zen Architects
0311, 0372, 0414
Franklin Azzi Architecture
www.franklinazzi.com
© Franklin Azzi Architecture
0312
Zhang Lei/AZL Architects
www.azlarchitects.com
© Nacasa & Partners
0313 (0070)
0314 (0026)
0315 (0042)
0316 (0175)
0317 (0018)
0318, 0397
Álvaro Ramírez, Clarisa Elton
www.ramirez-moletto.cl
© Álvaro Ramírez, Clarisa Elton, Carlos Ferrer
0319 (0134)
0320
GAD Architecture
http://gadarchitecture.com
© Ali Bekman, Ozlem Ercil

0321 (0017)
0322
Ronan & Erwan Bouroullec
www.bouroullec.com
© Paul Tahon and Ronan & Erwan Bouroullec
0323 (0016)
0324 (0070)
0325 (0126)
0326 (0269)
0327
Siris/Coombs Architects
www.siriscoombs.com
© Durston Saylor
0328, 0684, 0687, 0668, 0695
Maria Almirall, Ramón Robusté
maria_almirall@coac.net
© Despacho Maria Almirall
0329 (0125)
0330 (0111)
0331 (0042)
0332 (0196)
0333, 0423, 0508
Mikan
www.mikan.co.jp
© Covi
0334 (0125)
0335 (0281)
0336 (0227)
0337, 0558
Takaharu & Yui Tezuka/Tezuka Architects, Masahiro Ikeda/
Masahiro Ikeda Co.
www.masahiroikeda.com
© Katsuhisa Kida
0338 (0138)
0339 (0038)
0340 (0021)
0341, 0405
Edward Suzuki Associates
www.edward.net
© Yasuhiro Nukamura
0342 (0080)
0343 (0092)
0344 (0128)
0345 (0222)
0346 (0147)
0347, 0609
Rafael Berkowitz
rafael.berkowitz@verizon.net
© James Wilkins (0347)
© Rafael Berkowitz (0609)
0348
Kutschker Leischner Architekten
www.k-l-architekten.de
© Kutschker Leischner Architekten
0349 (0134)
0350 (0013)
0351
BBP Architects
www.bbparchitects.com
© Cristopher Ott
0352, 0375, 0376, 0490, 0916, 0918, 0919, 0923
Andres Remy Arquitectos
http://andresremy.com
© Alejandro Peral, Gustavo Sosa Pinilla (0352)
© Alejandro Peral, Juan Raña (0375, 0916)
© Alejandro Peral (0376, 0490, 0919, 0923)
© Gustavo Sosa Pinilla (0918)
0353 (0102)
0354 (0271)
0355
María Victoria Besonías, Guillermo de Almeida, Luciano Kruk/BAK
Arquitectos
www.bakarquitectos.com.ar
© Gustavo Sosa Pinilla/Summa+

0356 (0023)
0357
Fougeron Architecture
www.fougeron.com
© Richard Barnes
0358 (0067)
0359 (0034)
0360 (0130)
0361 (0310)
0362 (0277)
0363 (0006)
0364 (0158)
0365 (0061)
0366
CSA Architects
www.csa-architects.co.uk
© Richard Powers
0367 (0136)
0368 (0069)
0369 (0002)
0370
Gavin Harris, Henrietta Reed/Mackay & Partners
www.mackayandpartners.co.uk
© Niall Clutton
0371, 0696
Shipley Architects
www.shipleyarchitects.com
© Charles Davis Smith
0372 (0311)
0373 (0242)
BUILD LLC
www.buildllc.com
© BUILD LLC
0374 (0013)
0375 (0352)
0376 (0352)
0377 (0045)
0378, 0752
Studio Granda
http://studiogranda.is
© Sigurgeir Sigurjónsson
0379 (0030)
0380 (0131)
0381 (0171)
0382 (0147)
0383, 0384, 0385, 0388, 0393, 0396, 0426, 0437, 0442, 0649
Arboretum
www.arboretum.es
© Jordi Jové
0384 (0383)
0385 (0383)
0386 (0090)
0387 (0556)
Jyrki Tasa
www.n-r-t.fi
© Jyrki Tasa
0388 (0383)
0389, 0400, 0418, 0424, 0468, 0656
Kettal
www.kettal.es
© Kettal
0390 (0222)
0391
Baumraum
www.baumraum.de
© Alasdair Jardine
0392
Roche Bobois
www.roche-bobois.com
© Roche Bobois
0393 (0383)

0394
Stanley Saitowitz/Natoma Architects
www.saitowitz.com
© Rien van Rijthoven
0395 (0138)
0396 (0383)
0397 (0318)
0398
N.A.
© Marc Gerritsen
0399 (0082)
0400 (0389)
0401 (0310)
0402 (0076)
0403 (0217)
0404 (0171)
0405 (0341)
0406, 0744, 0764, 0876
Studio 804
www.studio804.com
© Courtesy of Studio 804
0407
Cary Bernstein
www.cbstudio.com
© Sharon Risendorph
0408
Wingårdh Arkitektkontor
www.wingardhs.se
© Ulf Celander
0409, 0627, 0644, 0666
Shubin & Donaldson Architects
www.sandarc.com
© Ciro Cohelo
0410
Fantastic Norway Architects
http://fantasticnorway.no
© Fantastic Norway Architects
0411, 0814, 0900, 0902
Solares Architecture, Inc
www.solares.ca
© Solares Architecture, Inc
0412 (0061)
0413 (0214)
0414 (0311)
0415 (0188)
0416 (0023)
0417, 0474, 0933, 0955
Edward Szewczyk + Associates Architects
www.esa-architect.com.au
© Michael Saggus, Edward Szewczyk (0417, 0474, 0933)
© Michael Saggus (0955)
0418 (0389)
0419
Paul Archer Architects
www.paularcherdesign.co.uk
© Paul Smoothy
0420 (0026)
0421, 0449, 0636
Leroy Street Studio Architecture
www.leroystreetstudio.com
© Adrian Wilson
0422, 0430
Kenji Tagashira
www.kenji-tagashira.com
© Kei Sugino
0423 (0333)
0424 (0389)
0425
Höweler & Yoon Architecture
www.hyarchitecture.com
© Höweler & Yoon Architecture
0426 (0383)
0427 (0254)
0428 (0052)

0429, 0987
Suppose Design Office
www.suppose.jp
© Toshiyuki Yano, Nacása & Partners (0429)
© Nacása & Partners (0987)
0430 (0422)
0431
N.A.
© Jovan Horvath
0432
NIP Paysage
www.nippaysage.ca
© NIP Paysage
0433
N.A.
© Kouji Okamoto
0434
N.A.
© Paolo Utimpergher
0435
Patricia Urquiola
www.patriciaurquiola.com
© Kettal
0436 (0134)
0437 (0383)
0438, 0453
Rios Clementi Hale Studios
www.rchstudios.com
© John Ellis
0439
Jane Hamley Wells
www.janehamleywells.com
© Jane Hamley Wells
0440 (0160)
0441
N.A.
© Ricardo Labougle
0442 (0383)
0443 (0155)
0444
N.A.
© Phillippe Saharof
0445
Extremis
www.extremis.be
© Extremis
0446
N.A.
© Ian Bradshaw
0447 (0576)
Miro Rivera Architects
www.mirorivera.com
© Patrick Wong
0448 (0277)
0449 (0421)
0450
N.A.
© Michael Freeman
0451 (0087)
0452, 0469
Rotzler Krebs Partner
www.rotzler-krebs.ch
© Rotzler Krebs Partner
0453 (0438)
0454
TOPOS Atelier
www.toposatelier.com
© Xavier Antunes
0455 (0165)
0456
Raderschall
www.raderschall.ch
© Raderschall

0457
N.A.
© Michael Freeman
0458
John Cunningham Architects, Landworks Studio, Office DA
www.landworksstudio.com
© Landworks Studio
0459 (0161)
0460 (0071)
0461 (0111)
0462
Bensley Design Studios
www.bensley.com
© Bensley Design Studios
0463
N.A.
© Casamanía
0464
Andrea Cochran
www.acochran.com
© Andrea Cochran
0465 (0196)
0466
N.A.
© Michael Freeman
0467
HyoMan Kim/IROJE KHM Architects
www.irojekhm.com
© MoonJeaonsSik
0468 (0389)
0469 (0452)
0470
GARDENA
www.gardena.com
© GARDENA
0471
N.A.
© John Ellis
0472 (0124)
0473
Verzone Woods Architectes
www.vwa.ch
© Verzone Woods Architectes
0474 (0417)
0475
N.A.
© Chipper Hatter
0476 (0581)
Japan Landscape Consultants
www.kenkohji.jp
© Japan Landscape Consultants
0477 (0277)
0478
LAR/Fernando Romero
www.fr-ee.org
© Paul Czitrom, Luis Gordoa, Jorge Silva
0479, 0637, 0883
Arkhefield with Shaun Lockyer
www.arkhefield.com.au
© Scott Burrows
0480 (0285)
0481 (0196)
0482 (0050)
0483, 0942
Hariri & Hariri Architecture
www.haririandhariri.com
© Paul Warchol
0484 (0282)
0485 (0541)
N.A.
© Aiko Mitsubishi
0486 (0196)

0487 (0577)
N.A.
© Dan Magree
0488, 0584
Eduardo Cadaval & Clara Solà-Morales
www.ca-so.com
© Cadaval Solà-Morales (0488)
© Santiago Garcés, Cadaval Solà-Morales (0584)
0489
JM Architecture
www.jma.it
© Gasser. Jacopo Mascheroni
0490 (0352)
0491
Design Worldwide Partnership
www.dwp.com
© Amir Sultan
0492
Asian Motifs
www.asianmotifs.com
© Asian Motifs
0493
New ID Interiors
www.new-id.co.uk
© Carlos Domínguez
0494
N.A.
© John M. Hall, Francesc Zamora
0495
Rocío Fueyo
N.A.
© Jordi Miralles
0496
Entre4parets
www.entre4parets.com
© Sandra Pereznieto
0497, 0542
Alno
www.alno.be
© Alno, Hardy Inside (0497)
© Alno (0542)
0498
David Boyle
www.davidboylearchitect.com.au
© Murray Fredericks
0499
Kim Utzon Arkitekter
www.utzon-arkitekter.dk
© Carlos Cezanne
0500 (0188)
0501
N.A.
© Ángel Baltanás, Francesc Zamora
0502 (0030)
0503
Fabrizio Miccò
http://fmaa.it
© Beatrice Pediconi
0504
N.A.
© Ernesto Meda
0505
Paik & Holtzer
www.paik-holtzer.com
© Mikiko Kukiyama
0506, 0509
Jamie Fobert Architects
www.jamiefobertarchitects.com
© David Grandorge
0507 (0024)
0508 (0333)
0509 (0506)

0510
N.A.
© Marcelo Nunes, Sue Barr, Francesc Zamora
0511
Anima LLC Architecture & Design
www.anima.cc
© Anima LLC Architecture & Design
0512 (0074)
0513 (0072)
0514 (0047)
0515 (0024)
0516 (0128)
0517, 0524, 0648
Carlo Dal Bianco
www.carlodalbianco.it
© Ottavio Tomasini
0518 (0017)
0519, 0573
Philippe Starck YOO LTD CF Møller/Pertner Lone Wiggers
www.yoo.com
© YOO
0520, 0623
Camezind Evolution
www.camenzindevolution.com
© Camezind Evolution
0521 (0192)
0522, 0523
Studio Gaia
www.studiogaia.com
© Moon Lee
0523 (0522)
0524 (0517)
0525
N.A.
© Tuca Reinés, Francesc Zamora
0526 (0047)
0527, 0566
Alan Barr, Bree Dahl
N.A.
© Eric Laignel
0528 (0047)
0529 (0070)
0530 (0047)
0531
Marco Savorelli
www.sa-architecture.it
© Matteo Piazza
0532
Tang Kawasaki Studio
www.tangkawasaki.com
© Andrea Morini
0533 (0024)
0534 (0039)
0535, 0721, 0727, 0728
Carola Vannini Architecture
www.carolavannini.com
© Filipo Vinardi
0536 (0068)
0537 (0173)
0538 (0290)
0539 (0096)
0540 (0173)
0541
Kimmo Friman/friman.laaksonen arkkitehdit Oy
www.fl-a.fi
© Rauno Träskelin
0542 (0497)
0543 (0013)
0544 (0039)
0545, 0571, 0572
Karim Rashid
www.karimrashid.com
© Jean François Jussaud

0652, 0671
Gandía Blasco
www.gandiablasco.com
© Gandía Blasco
0653 (0132)
0654
Mariano Martín
www.marianomartin.com
© Mariano Martín
0655
Guerrilla Office Architects
www.g-o-a.be
© goa
0656 (0389)
0657 (0578)
0658 (0132)
0659
Pascal Arquitectos
www.pascalarquitectos.com
© Sófocles Hernández
0660 (0167)
0661 (0634)
0662 (0159)
0663 (0167)
0664 (0592)
0665 (0606)
Bloom!
www.bloomholland.nl
© Bloom!
0666 (0409)
0667 (0069)
0668 (0069)
0669 (0030)
0670 (0592)
0671 (0652)
0672 (0549)
0673
Santa & Cole
www.santacole.com
© Santa & Cole
0674 (0012)
0675
Plust Collection
www.plust.it
© Plust Collection
0676 (0574)
0677
Stefano Merlo
www.stefanomerlo.com
© Curzio Castellan
0678 (0634)
0679
Holodeck Architects
www.holodeckarchitects.com
© Ike Branco
0680 (0619)
0681
Hulger
www.hulger.com
© Hanna Jeffery
0682
Demakersvan
www.demakersvan.com
© Ingmar Cramers
0683
Felix Stark for FORMSTARK
www.formstark.com
© Formstark
0684 (0328)
0685, 0689, 0691
Gianpaolo Benedini/Benedini Architetti
http://benedinipartners.it
© Franco Marconcini

0686 (0629)
0687 (0328)
0688 (0328)
0689 (0685)
0690 (0158)
0691 (0685)
0692 (0262)
0693 (0634)
0694 (0033)
0695 (0328)
0696 (0371)
0697 (0147)
0698 (0140)
0699 (0153)
0700
Henning Stummel Architects
www.henningstummelarchitects.co.uk
© Luke Caufield, Nigel Rigden
0701 (0134)
0702 (0155)
0703, 0898
Change Architect
www.changearchitect.com
© Pieter Kers/Change Architects
0704
Andy Macdonald/Mac-Interactive Architecture
www.mac-interactive.com
© Romain Machefer
0705
Nobbs Radford Architecture
http://nobbsradford.com.au
© Petter Bennets
0706
Sanya Polescuk Architects
www.polescukarchitects.com
© Ioana Marinescu
0707
Stelle Architects
www.stelleco.com
© Michael Lomont
0708 (0020)
0709, 0808, 0870
Marmol Radziner (0709)
Marmol Radziner Prefab (0808, 0870)
www.marmol-radziner.com
http://marmolradzinerprefab.com
© David Glomb (0709)
© Tyler Boye (0808, 0870)
0710 (0611)
0711
Driendl Architects
http://driendl.at
© Driendl Architects
0712, 0713
Yiorgos Hadjichristou
www.yiorgoshadjichristou.com
© Papantoniou, Y. Hadjichristou , Y. Kordakis
0713 (0712)
0714
Atelier KS
http://atelier-ks.com
© Atelier KS
0715
Mattinson Associates
www.mattinsonassociates.co
© N.A.
0716, 0731, 0940
Alla Kazovsky
www.designedrealestate.com
© Josh Perrin
0717
Labics
www.labics.it
© Luigi Filetici

0718 (0262)
0719
BOB361 Architects
www.bob361.com
© BOB361 Architects
0720
Tom Ferguson Architecture and Design
www.tfad.com.au
© Simon Kenny/Content
0721 (0535)
0722 (0258)
0723
Jeffrey McKean Architect
www.jeffreymckean.com
© Keith Mendenhall
0724
Estilo Arquitectura
www.estiloyucatan.com
© Roberto Cárdenas Cabello
0725
Nacho Polo
www.nachopolo.com
© Antonio Terron, Andrea Savini
0726
Despang Architekten
www.despangarchitekten.de
© Olaf Baumann
0727 (0535)
0728 (0535)
0729
Josep Maria Esquius Prat
+34 938 720 888
© Lourdes Jansana
0730 (0097)
0731 (0716)
0732
Eric Gartner, Coty Sidnam/SPG Architects
www.spgarchitects.com
© Charles Lindsay
0733 (0034)
0734, 0779, 0781, 0830, 0866, 0885
Obie G. Bowman
www.obiebowman.com
© Obie G. Bowman (0734, 0779, 0866)
© Obie G. Bowman, Robert Foothorap (0781, 0830, 0885)
0735 (0088)
0736 (0107)
0737 (0014)
0738 (0119)
0739, 0868
David Lorente, Josep Ricart, Xavier Ros, Roger Tudó/H Arquitectes
http://harquitectes.com
© Starp Estudi
0740
Pugh & Scarpa
www.pugh-scarpa.com
© Marvin Rand
0741
N.A.
© Guillermo Pffaf
0742 (0088)
0743, 0810, 0871, 0882
Michelle Kaufmann
http://michellekaufmann.com
© John Swain
0744 (0406)
0745, 0901
University of Illinois
http://illinois.edu
© University of Illinois
0746
Pich-Aguilera Arquitectos
www.picharchitects.com
© Pich-Aguilera Arquitectos

0747, 0767, 0768, 0899
Martin Liefhebber/Breathe Architects
www.breathebyassociation.com
© Martin Liefhebber
0748
Chromagen
http://chromagen.es
© Chromagen
0749
© Jorgeantonio/Dreamstime.com
0750
N.A.
© Saunier Duval
0751, 0784, 0831, 0880, 0908
Arkin Tilt Architects
www.arkintilt.com
© Edward Caldwell
0752 (0378)
0753
Peter Cardew Architects
www.cardew.ca
© Peter Cardew, Sarah Murray
0754
N.A.
© Guillermo Pffaf
0755
Soliclima
www.soliclima.es
© Soliclima
0756 (0110)
0757
N.A.
© Guillermo Pffaf
0758
Luca Lancini/Fujy
www.lucalancini.com
© Miguel de Guzmán
0759, 0783
Architectenbureau Paul de Ruiter bv
www.paulderuiter.nl
© Pieter Kers
0760
Minarc Architects
www.minarc.com
© Erla Dögg Ingjaldsdóttir, Ralph Seeberger, Bragi Joseffson
0761
Ecospace
www.ecospacestudios.com
© Ecospace
0762
Ken Fowler, Michael Rea
www.esd.co.uk
www.zerocarbonhouse.com
© Ken Fowler, Michael Rea
0763
Home Energy International
www.home-energy.com
© Home Energy International
0764 (0406)
0765
Sonkyo Energy, Weole Energy
www.sonkyogroup.com
© Sonkyo Energy, Weole Energy
0766, 0770, 0821, 0825
Simon Winstanley Architects
www.candwarch.co.uk
© Simon Winstanley Architects
0767 (0747)
0768 (0747)
0769
N.A.
© Guillermo Pffaf
0770 (0766)

0771
N.A.
© Guillermo Pffaf
0772 (0090)
0773, 0775, 0817, 0836, 0864, 0867
Max Pritchard Architect
www.maxpritchardarchitect.com.au
© Ben Della Torre (0773, 0864)
© Sam Noonan (0775, 0817, 0836, 0867)
0774 (0158)
0775 (0773)
0776 (0064)
0777 (0634)
0778
N.A.
© Guillermo Pffaf
0779 (0734)
0780, 0872
Kieran Timberlake Associates
http://kierantimberlake.com
© Barry Halkin
0781 (0734)
0782, 0824
Casagrande Laboratory
www.clab.fi
© Casagrande Laboratory
0783 (0759)
0784 (0751)
0785 (0157)
0786 (0292)
0787, 0936, 0939
Denniston International Architects
www.denniston.com.my
© Marc Barbay (0787)
© Courtesy of Denniston (0936, 0939)
0788
Ray Kappe
www.livinghomes.net
www.kappedu.com
© CJ Berg
0789
Room 11 Studio PTY LTD
www.room11.com.au
© Jasmin Latona
0790
Choi Ropila
http://chrofi.com
© Simon Whitbread, Choi Ropila
0791 (0277)
0792 (0126)
0793 (0158)
0794 (0153)
0795
Dorte Mandrup Architects Aps
www.dortemandrup.dk
© Torben Eskerod
0796 (0222)
0797 (0171)
0798, 0815
EHDD Architecture
www.ehdd.com
© Doug Snower
0799, 0820
Florian Maurer/Allen + Maurer Architects Ltd.
www.allenmaurer.com
© Florian Maurer, Stuart Bish
0800
Christina Zerva Architects
www.christinazerva.com
© Mihajlo Savic
0801
Jordan
www.jordan-solar.at
© Andreas Buchberger

0802
Paul McKean Architecture
www.pmckean.com
© Paul McKean Architecture
0803, 0832
DecaArchitecture
www.deca.gr
© Erietta Attali, Ed Reeve, Julia Klimi, decaArchitecture
0804
N.A.
© Guillermo Pffaf
0805
Giovani D'Ambrosio
www.giovannidambrosio.com
© Giovani D'Ambrosio
0806 (0146)
0807
Tuomo Siitonen Architects
www.tsi.fi
© Rauno Träskelin, Mikko Auerniitty
0808 (0709)
0809
Francois Perrin
http://francoisperrin.com
© Michaels Wells, Joshua White
0810 (0743)
0811 (0142)
0812 (0021)
0813
Bruns Architecture
www.brunsarchitecture.com
© Bruns Architecture
0814 (0411)
0815 (0798)
0816 (0014)
0817 (0773)
0818 (0021)
0819
N.A.
© Guillermo Pffaf
0820 (0799)
0821 (0766)
0822 (0014)
0823, 0839
Una Arquitetos
www.unaarquitetos.com.br
© Bebete Viégas
0824 (0782)
0825 (0766)
0826 (0140)
0827
N.A.
© Guillermo Pffaf
0828, 0835
Taketo Shimohigoshi/A.A.E.
www.aae.jp
© Shigeo Ogawa, Koichi Torimura
0829
SSD Architecture + Urbanism
www.ssdarchitecture.com
© SSD Architecture + Urbanism
0830 (0734)
0831 (0751)
0832 (0803)
0833
R&Sie(n)
www.new-territories.com
© R&Sie(n)
0834 (0142)
0835 (0828)
0836 (0773)

0837
Morphosis
www.morphosis.com
© Iwan Baan
0838
N.A.
© Guillermo Pffaf
0839 (0823)
0840
Heliotrope
www.heliotropearchitects.com
© Benjamin Benschneider
0841 (0119)
0842
Nicholas Burns Associates
http://nicholas-burns.com
© Earl Carter
0843
Hansgrohe
www.hansgrohe.com
© Hansgrohe
0844
Gabriele Buratti, Oscar Buratti
www.burattibattiston.it
© Roca
0845
Ian Alexander
www.hughie.com.au
© Hughie
0846
N.A.
© Guillermo Pffaf
0847
Riches Hawley Mikhail Architects
www.rhmarchitects.com
© Tim Crocker, Nick Kane
0848
Correia/Ragazzi Arquitectos
www.correiaragazzi.com
© Alberto Plácido, Juan Rodríguez
0849
Marcadiferencia
www.marcadiferencia.com
© Marcadiferencia
0850, 0857
Tres
www.tresgriferia.com
© Tres
0851
Dubbeldam Design Architects
http://dubbeldamarchitects.com
© Shai Gil
0852
Dornbracht, MGS Designs
www.dornbracht.com
www.mgsdesigns.com
© Dornbracht, MGS Designs
0853, 0854, 0860, 0861
Orfesa
www.orfesa.net
© Orfesa (0853, 0860, 0861)
© Orfesa, Jordi Miralles (0854)
0854 (0853)
0855
Hansgrohe, Roca
www.hansgrohe.com
www.roca.com
© Hansgrohe, Roca
0856, 0859
Envirolet by Sancor Industries Ltd.
www.envirolet.com
© Envirolet by Sancor Industries Ltd.
0857 (0850)

0858
Grupo Irisana
www.irisana.com
© Grupo Irisana
0859 (0856)
0860 (0853)
0861 (0853)
0862
Marc Dixon
marcdixon@netspace.net.au
© Lucas Dawson
0863 (0045)
0864 (0773)
0865 (0171)
0866 (0734)
0867 (0773)
0868 (0739)
0869 (0270)
0870 (0709)
0871 (0743)
0872 (0780)
0873 (0270)
0874 (0028)
0875
Dietrich Schwarz
www.schwarz-architektur.ch
© Frédérik Comtesse
0876 (0406)
0877 (0034)
0878
© Amorim, Vatrux/Dreamstime.com
0879
© WWF/Canon N.C. Turner, Chachas/Dreamstime.com
0880 (0751)
0881
© Stepunk/Dreamstime.com, Mouton1980/Dreamstime.com, Tuka Bamboo
0882 (0743)
0883 (0479)
0884
© Pasi Aalto/TYIN tegnestue, ThreeHouse Company
0885 (0734)
0886
© Margouillat/Dreamstime.com
0887
© N.A.
0888
N.A.
© Gernot Minke
0889
N.A.
© Guillermo Pffaf
0890
© Reinhold68/Dreamstime.com
0891
N.A.
© Atelier Werner Schmidt, Catharine Wanek
0892 (0157)
0893
© Clearviewstock/Dreamstime.com
0894 (0165)
0895
N.A.
© Hannes Henz Architekturfotograf
0896
© Nalapic/Dreamstime.com, Danilo Ascione/Shutterstock.com
0897 (0260)
0898 (0703)
0899 (0747)
0900 (0411)
0901 (0745)
0902 (0411)

0903
Porcelanosa
www.porcelanosa.com
© Porcelanosa
0904 (0098)
0905
© Typhoonski/Dreamstime.com, Jeremy Philips
0906
Cannabric
www.cannabric.com
© Cannabric
0907
Leger Wanaselja Architecture
www.lwarc.com
© Cesar Rubio, Karl Wanaselja
0908 (0751)
0909, 0911
Piera Ecocerámica
www.pieraecoceramica.es
© Piera Ecocerámica
0910 (0098)
0911 (0909)
0912 (0202)
Javier Artadi/Artadi Arquitectos
www.javierartadi.com
© Alfio Garozzo
0913
Dardelet
www.dardelet.ch
© Dardelet
0914
Jungles Landscape Architecture
www.raymondjungles.com
© Lenny Provo
0915, 0949
Alberto Burckhardt
alburcart@yahoo.com
© Jean Marc Wullschleger
0916 (0352)
0917, 0929
Lutsko Associates
www.lutskoassociates.com
© Nicola Brown
0918 (0352)
0919 (0352)
0920 (0087)
0921 (0125)
0922
Bioteich
www.bioteich.fr
© Bioteich
0923 (0352)
0924, 0934
Joan Roca Vallejo
http://aquart.net
© Jordi Miralles
0925
N.A.
© Erik Saillet
0926 (0973)
Bedmar & Shi
www.bedmar-and-shi.com
© Bedmar & Shi
0927
Donald Jacob
www.jacob-planung.ch
© Donald Jacob
0928
Juan Robles, Andrea Solano, Emilio Quirós/Robles Arquitectos
www.roblesarq.com
© Robles Arquitectos
0929 (0917)
0930 (0060)

0931 (0160)
0932 (0169)
0933 (0417)
0934 (0924)
0935
Hidalgo Hartmann Arquitectura
www.hidalgohartmann.com
© Robert Prat Riera, Jordi Hidalgo
0936 (0787)
0937
Procter Rihl Architects
www.procter-rihl.com
© Marcelo Nunes, Sue Barr
0938
Designworkshop:SA
www.designworkshopsa.com
© Clinton Friedman
0939 (0787)
0940 (0716)
0941 (0147)
0942 (0483)
0943, 0946
Luigi Rosselli Architects
http://luigirosselli.com
© Richard Glover
0944
Klab Architects
www.klab.gr
© Klab Architects
0945 (0277)
0946 (0943)
0947
Marco Aldaco
http://marcoaldacodesigns.com
© Michael Gilbreath
0948
Ramon Esteve Estudio de Arquitectura
www.ramonesteve.com
© Xavier Mollà
0949 (0915)
0950, 0952
Lundberg Design
www.lundbergdesign.com
© Cesar Rubio (0950)
© JD Peterson (0952)
0951 (0165)
0952 (0950)
0953
Giuseppe Chigiotti
www.chigiotti-archlab.com
© Giuseppe Chigiotti
0954 (0168)
0955 (0417)
0956
Leopoldo Rosati
www.leopoldorosati.com
© Leopoldo Rosati
0957
Donald Billinkoff Architects
www.billinkoff.com
© Donald Martinez, Mark Samu, Elliot Kaufman
0958 (0589)
0959 (0168)
0960
Bárbara Andreu/CAD Interiorismo
+34 932 123 116
© Núria Fuentes
0961
Shinichi Ogawa & Associates
www.shinichiogawa.com
© Nácasa & Partners

0962
Aloha Pools Creative Outdoor Solutions
www.alohapools.com.au
© Tim Turner
0963
Guilhem Roustan
www.ateliernordsud.com
© Daniel Moulinet
0964, 0971
Marcel Wanders, Karin Krautgartner (0964)
Marcel Wanders Studio (0971)
www.marcelwanders.com
© Alberto Ferrero (0964)
© Marcel Wanders Studio (0971)
0965
N.A.
© Wetstyle, Acquatic
0966 (0047)
0967
Jaclo
www.jaclo.com
© Jaclo
0968 (0030)
0969
Ross Lovegrove for Vitra
www.rosslovegrove.com
© Vitra
0970 (0122)
0971 (0964)
0972, 0983
Bang & Olufsen
www.bang-olufsen.com
© Bang & Olufsen
0973 (0277)
0974
Roy Leone Design Studio
www.royleone.com
© Eduard Hueber/Archphoto
0975
Francesc Rifé
www.rife-design.com
© Gogortza & Llorella
0976
Scape Architects
www.scape-architects.com
© Michele Panzeri
0977, 0980
Werner
www.werner-musica.com
© Gogortza & Llorella
0978
Shadi Shahrokhi
www.shadiandcompany.com
© Andrea Morini
0979
Artcoustic
www.artcoustic.com
© Artcoustic
0980 (0977)
0981 (0110)
0982
Ajrapetov
N.A.
© The Interior Archive
0983 (0972)
0984, 0985
nARCHITECTS
www.narchitects.com
© Frank Oudeman
0985 (0984)
0986 (0120)
0987 (0429)

0988
Ramón Soler
www.ramonsoler.net
© Ramón Soler
0989
J. Mayer H. Architects
www.jmayerh.de
© Stuart McIntyre
0990
Coop Himmelblau
www.coop-himmelblau.at
© Gerald Zugmann
0991
Newform
www.newform.it
© Newform
0992, 0999
White Architects, White Design
http://white-design.com
© Bert Leanderson, Richard Lindor
0993
Paul + O Architects
www.paul-o-architects.com
© Fernando Guerra/FS + SG
0994 (0060)
0995 (0052)
0996
BURO II/BURO Interior
www.buro2.be
© Danica Ocvirk Kus, Kris Vandamme
0997
Luigi Colani, Hanse Haus
www.hanse-haus.de
© Hanse Haus GmbH
0998 (0292)
0999 (0992)
1000
Johnson Chou
www.johnsonchou.com
© Volker Seding Photography